Advanced Praise for

"A sweet, inspiring portrayal of ᵍ
ing, along with a simple, light-hearted - even fun - spiritual
practice for bringing more blessing into your life. Salvatore
Sapienza's *Gay is a Gift* is itself a gift."

-Toby Johnson, author of *Gay Spirituality*

"Think of *Gay is a Gift* as a Chicken Soup for the Gay Soul"
-*Web Digest Weekly*

Praise for *Seventy Times Seven*

"Required reading for gay persons of faith."
- *Q Media Syndicate*

"An important book, taking on spirituality and homosexuality.
This book is a victory for the Gay Spirit."
-Trebor Healey, author of *Through It Came Bright Colors*

"Deeply moving and reverent. Sapienza's book is the perfect
dose of medicine demonstrating that it's perfectly okay to be
both gay and a person of faith"   - *EDGE Magazine*

"Engaging, thoughtful, refreshingly honest."
IN L.A. Magazine

Lambda Literary Award Nominee:
BEST SPIRITUALITY

First Edition 2009

All Rights Reserved Copyright 2009
by Tregatti Press
Gay is a Gift

Tregatti Press
P.O. Box 2
Saugatuck, MI 49495

Published by Tregatti Press
www.tregattipress.com
www.gayisagift.com

Printed in the United States of America
Author Photo: Wyatt Lane

Gay is a Gift/Salvatore Sapienza

ISBN: 978-0-615-33904-7

1. Self-Help   2. Body, Mind & Spirit   I. Title
Gay is a Gift

Gay is a Gift

by Salvatore Sapienza

Tregatti Press

Dedicated to:

My parents,
whose unconditional love first made me aware of my
*GIFT*edness

My partner, Gregg,
who patiently stood by when I forgot it

and to Divine Spirit,
whose Grace reawakened me to it

"I'm here to **remind** you of your
magnificence

To help you **awake** to
all the **wonder** that you are

I long to show you all the **joy**
you're **worthy** of

I'm here to **remind** you just how much
you're **truly loved.**"

-David Ault

An Introduction

Remember those *Chicken Soup for the Soul* series of pocket-sized books? Co-created by Jack Canfield, one of the authors of the bestselling book *The Secret,* each book in the *Chicken Soup* series was a spiritual and motivational guide-book for the souls of a different group of people. There are over one hundred different titles in print, from *Chicken Soup for the Mother's Soul* to *Chicken Soup for the Preteen's Soul,* even *Chicken Soup for the Prisoner's Soul* and, believe it or not, two volumes of *Chicken Soup for the Horse Lover's Soul.*

As I've grown in Spirit, I have sought over the years for a *Chicken Soup*-type book for the Gay Soul, but to no avail, so I decided to write one myself. It's the book you're now reading.

I hope that *Guy is a Gift* will warm your soul and help you reconnect with your spirit and special giftedness. Modeling it after other gift-sized motivational tomes, like Richard Carlson's *Don't Sweat the Small Stuff,* Don Miguel Ruiz's *The Four Agreements,* and Neale Donald Walsch's *Recreat-*

ing Yourself, I've created this book to be, like those books, a pocket-sized devotional, if you will - a small book which can be easily picked up again and again to provide the inspiration and encouraging words we all need to hear from time to time, words which remind us of our Spiritual nature.

Mother Theresa once advised spiritual writer and gay man Henri Nouwen to write "very simply," she said, because people needed simple words to understand spiritual concepts. Readers would often tell Nouwen that he articulated for them something they already knew, but still needed to hear.

In that regard, the wisdom I'm about to share is simply written and nothing new. Throughout the course of history, this knowledge has been shared with the world by countless men and women, all of whom are much more eloquent and higher in consciousness than I, and it's also a wisdom you already possess.

So why should you even bother to read this book? Well, first off, of all the thousands of books out there, this one - without benefit of a major publisher or advertising - somehow found it's way to you, and there are no accidents in our perfectly-ordered Universe.

The best books have come to me this way. By best, I mean those that found me at a time when I needed them most. There they'd be in seat back pockets on an airplane, in the nightstand drawer of a motel, on a fifty-cent used book table at a small town flea market, or even arriving unsolicited in the mail.

I am certain that this book has found its way to you, as it was written with enthusiasm (meaning "the Divine within") and in Spirit (where inspiration derives), and, I believe, the Universe has led you to discover it for a profound reason which will later be revealed to you.

Though this wisdom is universal and can be gleaned from a multitude of sources, I am certain that you've been led to hear my story, and that it will, in turn, lead you to a greater peace and a deeper consciousness. Though you may have been exposed to some of these ideas before, you may under-stand them in a new way by hearing them told from my life's perspective and in my writing style. Whatever the reason, understand that the Universe knows that you are ready to hear these words in a new way and wants you to hear them right now in the form of this book.

Throughout my story, I will be quoting from those wise men and women who have already shared this knowl-edge with the world. These spiritual teachers are ancient Chi-nese philosophers, Buddhist monks, Hindi mystics, Catholic saints, and current day New Age writers. Though they've lived on various continents, in different centuries, and have led wildly divergent lives, every single one of them has the same exact message to share with you. As one of them, Eck-hart Tolle (the author of *The Power of Now* and *A New Earth*) writes, "All spiritual teachings originate from the same Source."

Some of the teachers quoted here, however, are reli-gious figures, and that - for whatever reasons from your past - may make you uncomfortable and resistant. Don't let your ego (which we'll talk more of later) convince you that their teachings do not hold any relevance towards helping you grow in awareness simply because they were or are part of organized religious organizations.

Along the way, I will also share with you a bit about my own life. Although everyone's journey is different, I be-lieve that the primary reason for our existence is the process of expanding awareness in ourselves and in the world. So, I hope that the intermittent stories of my own life's journey will resonate, affirm and, ideally, inspire your own growing awareness of the Spirit, the same Spirit which resides in all of us and unites us all.

About the Book's Cover

The gift box on the book's front cover represents you and your giftedness, of course. The feathers rising from the box symbolize your ascension and spiritual evolution.

Native American spiritual leaders (the gay men who were referred to as "Two Spirits") wore feathers to express their celestial wisdom and symbolize their communication with Spirit, and the great medieval mystic, Hildegard of Bingen, whom some see as a lesbian saint, referred to herself as "a feather on the breath of God."

As for the gold star on the front of the book, well, that symbolizes guidance and light. The star has long been a symbol of guidance throughout the ages, and I hope the star on your gift will symbolize your finding the Divine Light within yourself.

Like that star, you are nothing but Light. Let your Starlight shine forth from the center to each point - from within to without - gracing the world around you with your very special Gift. Your Gay Gift.

Throughout the book, I use the word "gay" to encompass all gay, lesbian, bisexual, transgender and questioning people, yet I'm fully aware that it's impossible to fully capture the scope of our community with just this one word.

"My own guess is that homosexuals offer humanity certain vital gifts that society would be foolish to refuse."

- Matthew Fox

Gay Is A Gift From God

In January of 2009, Oprah Winfrey devoted an hour of her daytime talk show to exploring spirituality. Titled "Spirituality 101," the episode featured a panel of spiritual teachers, including Reverend Ed Bacon, a rector of All Saints Episcopal Church in Pasadena, California.

During the broadcast, the panel answered questions from audience members and those video-conferencing from home. One of those home callers, a 33 year old gay man from Atlanta named Sedrick, explained how growing up in a Christian home in rural Alabama caused him to see his sexuality as a hindrance in developing a fulfilling spiritual life.

In response, Reverend Bacon said simply and lovingly, "Being gay is a gift from God."

To put it mildly, Sedrick was taken aback, as if he was hearing a Divine revelation, and, indeed, he was. Oprah, herself, reacted with a look of surprise and astonishment at the reverend's declaration. "Well, you are the first minister I've ever heard say being gay is a gift from God, I can tell you that," Winfrey said, but her shock was delight, not disgust.

Another panelist, Michael Bernard Beckwith, founder and spiritual director of Agape International Spiritual Center in Los Angeles, then chimed in his response.

"We're not talking religion," Beckwith explained, "we're talking spirituality. People don't just happen to be gay. When people are born, they have that type of orientation, so he (Sedrick) is gay by Divine right."

Both Bacon and Beckwith got much flack from Oprah's online community, as hundreds of negative comments were posted on her show's website.

One viewer wrote, "I was watching this show this afternoon and immediately started praying. I cannot believe that two men, considered to be men of God and spiritual leaders, were completely misrepresenting what God has taught us through his Word! I feel so horrible for the young man who sought their guidance because now he is leaving this show with a sense that God approves of his lifestyle."

Another wrote, "I too was shocked at the 'minister' saying that being gay was a gift from God. I am disappointed that Oprah did not speak up, because I don't believe that she believes that. I have been disappointed in a lot of her shows. She has so much influence, and if she would use it in the right way, she could reach so many people. I believe she really does know the right path. She needs our prayers."

Throughout her career, Oprah Winfrey has done much to help her audience grow in consciousness through her thoughtful show topics and inspiring book club selections. One of the most prominent of the latter was her trumpeting of Eckhart Tolle's book *A New Earth*. Her multiple broadcasts on the book and her series of worldwide podcasts with the author helped propel the book to bestseller status, but, more importantly, it helped many people come to a better understanding of how to awaken to a new state of consciousness and to follow the path to a more peaceful and fulfilling life.

In Tolle's pervious book, *The Power of Now*, he addressed the question of gays and enlightenment at length.

When asked, "In the quest for enlightenment, is being gay a help or a hindrance, or does it make any difference?" Tolle responds that, yes, being gay "places you at an advantage as far as enlightenment is concerned."

He goes on to explain that the sense of being "different" from others forces gay people to misidentify with many of the socially conditioned patterns of thought and behavior which often impede spiritual growth.

"This will automatically raise your level of consciousness above that of the unconscious majority, whose members unquestioningly take on board all inherited patterns," Tolle writes. "(Being gay) takes you out of unconsciousness almost by force."

Decades before Tolle, the philosopher Carl Jung was also in agreement. He hypothesized that gays are often endowed with a spiritual receptivity that makes them responsive to revelation.

Gay is a gift is a wisdom the Native Americans knew centuries ago. In his book, *The Hidden Spirituality of Men*, spiritual writer and teacher Matthew Fox writes that "it is well known among Native Americans that gay persons have always been the spiritual directors to their great chiefs. Homosexuals, it seems, don't just bridge the male and female worlds, but human and spiritual worlds."

A Lakota shaman tells Fox that gay people have a gift of prophecy, explaining that "if nature put a burden on a man by making him different, it also gives him a power."

It is not just the Lakotas, but mostly all the Native American tribal cultures, it seems, have recognized gay people as holding special powers of the Spirit, giving them the title of Berdache or "Two Spirit." It is believed that these Two Spirits are more in tuned with the healing powers of natural beauty, and that they are the true Way Showers to the Divine Spirit.

It is no surprise to me, then, that gay people today are intrinsically drawn to vocations where they can use those same special powers. Think about it: there are disproportionately large numbers of gay people who are working as nurses, teachers, social workers, holistic healers, and in the arts.

This gay gift has been used throughout history in the creation of architecture, musical compositions, sculptures and paintings, poetry and prose, all of which have honored and celebrated the Divine.

Think about the lives and works of gay men and women throughout world history. People like Michelangelo, Leonardo da Vinci, George Frideric Handel, Tchaikovsky, Walt Whitman, Dag Hammarskjold, James Baldwin, Florence Nightingale, Virginia Woolf, Cole Porter, Rudolph Nurevey, Audre Lorde, Philip Johnson, Leonard Bernstein, George Gershwin, Stephen Sondheim, Bayard Rustin, Mychal Judge and Gertrude Stein, to name just a few.

It's no wonder then that humorist Sam Austin has joked, "Homosexuality is God's way of insuring that the truly gifted aren't burdened with children."

We are keepers of history, too, not only as museum directors, but as restorers. Gay people have often been the ones to venture into older historic neighborhoods that have long been forgotten, and have brought them back to life, preserving their history and their spirit.

And, however frivolous it may now seem, the television show "Queer Eye For the Straight Guy" made such an impact when it first aired, because at its heart, the five gay superheroes were using their powers (their gay gift) to improve the lives and spirits of straight men. The reason many of their straight male subjects got so emotional by show's end wasn't because their hair, clothes and apartments had transformed, but because their lives and spirits were, as well. (By the way, I always thought that the fifth Queer Eye guy, who never really had much to do, should have been a spiritual expert).

Decorating, grooming and fashion may seem trivial, but improving the lives of others is not. Oprah Winfrey's openly gay home decorating guru, Nate Berkus or team members from the "Extreme Makeover: Home Edition" television show may not be saving the world, but their gifts have changed the lives of those whose homes were destroyed by Hurricane Katrina, making their new dwellings places which bring spirits back to life.

The gay gift is one of compassion, creativity, affection, humor, acceptance, and hospitality. Many of us as children were deemed "sensitive," as if this was a bad thing. Today, we can see that our sensitivity is not a weakness, but one of the strengths of our gay gift.

Carl Jung believed that it was the balance of the masculine and feminine that caused the gift of creativity in the gay community. There may be a need in heterosexuals to find a partner of the opposite sex to complete this balance in order to feel whole and pro*create*, but Jung believed that gay people were already whole (the Native Americans said these were "holy" men) and, therefore, had the innate gift of creativity inside them.

We may not be able to procreate like heterosexuals, but we are pros at creating, aren't we?

Of course, gay people are working in every type of vocation from politicians to professional athletes, from ministers to mechanics, from teachers to tech-heads. That said, I do believe gay people have been given unique gifts - not better, but special powers - that help bring beauty, grace, artistry, compassion and spirit to a world in desperate need of them.

Jay Spears, webmaster of the site Gay Heroes, states it beautifully, "A feeling of being 'different' is one of the keys to genius, and gay people should know that many of history's great geniuses felt just the way they do. They show us that gay people can invoke eternal expressions of love, show us the amazing grace of God, create the most magnificent expressions of Christianity in painting, sculpture, architecture, and music. Everyone should be aware that gay and lesbian people are an important part of the magnificence of the human experience."

And, in his book, *Gay Spirit*, gay writer Mark Thompson says, "I would define gay people as possessing a luminous quality of being, a differentness that accentuates the gifts of compassion, empathy, healing, interpretation, and enabling. I see gay people as the in-between ones; those who can entertain irreconcilable differences, who are capable of uniting opposing forces as one; bridge builders who intuit the light and dark in all things."

If all this is true, and I believe it is, then how did we get to the place today where Sedrick and countless other gay people have failed to recognize themselves as holy (whole-y) men and women, have failed to embrace their roles as Way Showers? How did we lose touch with our giftedness, and, more importantly, how can we reconnect with it?

"There is a unique spiritual point of view that comes with being gay. This unique gift doesn't make us 'special' or 'superior,' but it is unique, and this gift is much needed."
                                    - gay artist, Peter Grahame

Gift of the Rainbow

Has someone ever given you a present that you just didn't like or didn't want? I think most of us can relate to that.

I remember that for my twelfth birthday my grandmother crocheted me a winter hat and matching scarf and gloves. She used as a multitude of colored yarns, as she couldn't remember the color of my winter coat and wanted to make sure that her creation would go with everything.

Though I politely thanked her upon receiving the gift, I knew that I would never wear it. As a young man struggling to comes to terms with his sexuality, I feared that wearing the multi-colored hat, scarf and gloves would make me look "gay" in front of my peers, so her gift sat unused on a shelf in my closet, because I was too ashamed to wear it out in public.

With the birthday money I received from various aunts and uncles, I went and purchased myself a Walkman, as this was the gift I really wanted for my birthday, mostly because every other kid at school had one.

Today, I have no need for that obsolete Walkman, but, oh, how I wish I still had my late Grandmother's gift. Hers was a gift of love, made specially for me with her own two hands, but I rejected it at the time in favor of a materialistic gift I selfishly gave myself, thinking, of course, that I knew better.

Looking at it now with adult eyes - and with Grandma long gone from this earthly plane - I now see how foolish I was to reject her gift. At the time she made it, she was elderly and couldn't walk well or stand for extended periods of time. Since she sat for most of the day, knitting was one of the few things she could still do to feel productive and to contribute to her family.

Oh, if I could only have that rainbow hat, scarf and gloves back today, they would be my most cherished gifts, and I'd wear them with pride, happy if they made me look "gay," for the rainbow is now the symbol of gay pride.

The Spirit of Love worked through Grandma's hands and brought into creation a gift which fit me perfectly, though it was the last thing I wanted at the time. Somehow, Grandma and Divine Spirit knew what was best for me.

Though I - and the gay community - have come a long way since I was twelve, there are still many gay people today who initially reject the gift they've been given. They reject the Gift of Gay, much as I rejected the gift from Grandma. Sure, they can try putting this gift on a closet shelf and try to forget about it. Or they can try exchanging it for something else, something more socially acceptable. They can even write "Return to Sender" on it and try to send it back.

The Sender, however, is Divine Wisdom, which always knows what's best for us, so it's foolish for us to deny this very special and holy gift which has been bestowed upon us.

As history attests, those who have rejected their gift-edness have led joyless existences and unfulfilled lives, but those who have joyfully accepted and utilized their rainbow gifts have always been rewarded with abundance and peace, for they are responding whole-heartedly to the Spirit within.

The rainbow is the perfect symbol for our gay gift. A rainbow is caused by the refraction or bending of light. (Have you ever heard the term "Bent" to refer to gay people?). Well, our gift as gay people is to be Light Workers - to display the full spectrum of colors that make up the sun's white light. As the sun sustains life, some have referred to it as the Living Light of God-ness or Good-ness.

Some view the arc of the rainbow as the symbol of a bridge between earth (human) and heaven (Spirit). Rainbows appear just twice in the Bible, in the beginning (Genesis) and the end (Revelation) of the book, and in each instance, it symbolizes a covenant between God and man.

The seven colors which make up the rainbow are different wavelengths of the one true Light. Interestingly enough, these seven colors also correspond with the seven chakra centers in the human body. Chakras are force or energy centers (often referred as vortexes or wheels of light) that are considered focal points for the reception and transmission of energy, or connection with the Light.

Each chakra center in the body is associated with a different color of the rainbow. Remember as a kid when you used the pneumonic device "Roy G. Biv" to help you remember the colors of the rainbow in order? Red, Orange, Yellow, Green, Blue, Indigo, Violet. Well, the chakra colors work the same way, from red up to violet.

These energy centers start at the anus (the "base chakra," which is the color red and symbolizes our groundedness or connectedness to earth) and then up through the body, ultimately culminating at the top of the head with the color violet (a color often associated with gay people) representing the "crown chakra," which is the chakra of pure consciousness or connectedness to the Divine.

Light is energy. It is all around us, though we can only see a small part of it with our visible eyes. It is in the essence of all living things from the stars to the sea. All light energy is frequency, and the different rainbow colors represent different frequencies of the same Light.

If we truly and fully embrace our Gay Gift as Rainbow Workers, we can indeed connect to this Light and bring about a higher consciousness for ourselves and, in turn, help awaken the consciousness of the world. This is our Divine calling and mission.

"We are healers, teachers, shamans, keepers of beauty, mediators and peacekeepers. Being gay is a gift, a blessing and a privilege." - Christian de la Huerta

<u>Embracing Our Gift</u>

We've seen the reasons why so many of us initially rejected our Gay Giftedness, but as we learn to not only accept but to embrace our gift, we begin to see how magnificent this gift really is. This is why so many of us look back and say how we wish we had come out of the closet sooner.

Being gay enables us to experience the world in more freeing and accepting manner. While many heterosexuals consider their family members to be their parents, siblings, and children, many gay people - who have been rejected by their biological families - have come to a different and more inclusive understanding of family.

Our families encompass neighbors and friends from very diverse backgrounds and life experiences. This sense of community extends far beyond our nuclear families, providing us with a much broader world view. Recognizing our Oneness with all is what most spiritual teachers say is the key to Enlightenment. Maybe that's why we have such an advantage here.

We also feel less of a need to look for a spouse in order to feel complete, nor are we burdened by the *Men Are From Mars, Women Are From Venus* conflicts between the male and female ways of seeing the world. Instead, we are more in balance with the yin and yang within us, which signifies harmony.

Those of us without children demonstrate that humans can live fulfilling and whole lives without reproducing, thereby sending a necessary message to an overpopulated world.

In fact, many of us without children may actually live lives much more "in the present," because we are not burdened by thoughts and worries of providing for our children and their futures. This freedom also allows us to more easily leave jobs which are not spiritually satisfying and to move about more freely and experience life in different places throughout the globe.

Those of us with children are often those who have provided loving homes for children who are not biologically ours. Because of our differentness, we feel less intimidated by - and sometimes more drawn to - caring for children who are from different races or who have special needs. We help raise society's "unwanted" children.

The planning and preparation involved when some gay couples do chose to have children biologically is often much more intensive and well thought out, especially in a world of numerous unplanned and unwanted pregnancies by heterosexual couples.

The same holds true for our quest for marriage equality. Countless heterosexual couples have run off to Las Vegas and have been married on a whim, a spur of the moment decision, yet gay couples who have been together for decades cannot have their unions legally recognized. The struggle for this legislation shows how seriously we take our relationships and the institution of marriage.

As we've also touched on, our gay gift draws many of us to the helping professions, as our "otherness" often makes us more sensitive to the needs of others. Our kind and caring nature is one of this gift's biggest benefits, for it benefits not only us, but everyone around us. Our gift gifts the entire world.

Am I being stereotypical here when I list our gay qualities? Some of you, for example, may be reading this section and thinking, "Well, I know some gay people who are selfish, unkind, and egotistical. You can't paint all of us with such a broad brush." While that is true, I do believe that certain commonalities exist among our very diverse gay community, just as there are defining traits among people in other communities and cultures.

For example, I am from Italian descent, and while there are some in the Italian culture who are like the characters on the TV series *The Sopranos*, the majority have gifted the world with familial affection and a zest for life. The mobsters may have forgotten those gifts, but they're there for the uncovering.

I feel the same way about our gay culture. Some of us have forgotten our giftedness. The purpose of this book is to help us remember.

"Homosexuals are the gatekeepers. Gatekeepers are people who live a life at the edge between two worlds - the world of the village and the world of the spirit."
- African writer and spiritual teacher, Sobonfu Somé

<u>Gays as Gatekeepers</u>

We have been given our gay giftedness by Divine right and for a Divine reason: It is our gift to the world.

As we have already discussed, gay people throughout history have used the gay gift to beautify the world through art, music, design, fashion and by gentrifying decaying neighborhoods, but we have also contributed greatly to improving the lives and spirits of our non-gay brothers and sisters.

Through coming to terms with our sexuality and ultimately coming out of the closet, gay people have experienced a sexual freedom many heterosexual people have not. We feel comfortable expressing our sexuality and discussing sexual issues openly.

The popular television series and movie *Sex and the City* has been considered ground-breaking and revolutionary for getting many straight women to speak about their sexual needs and desires for the first time. That series, however, was created and written by gay men.

Many straight women say they can more easily confide with a close gay male friend than they can with their girl-friends or spouses, especially when it comes to discussing sexual issues. The "gay best friend" has almost becoming a stock character in most romantic comedy movies today.

Straight men, too, have benefited from witnessing our sexual expression. Many heterosexual men have now begun to embrace their *metrosexual* sides, and they're getting more comfortable with expressing what were once considered feminine pursuits, like taking an interest in grooming and fashion, and by becoming more sensitive to the needs of their partners. We, as gay people, have modeled these qualities for them.

And, like many of the most important spiritual teachers in human history, gay people today continue to challenge many long-established and antiquated religious convictions, and we help open hearts and minds to new ideas and ways of seeing. We demonstrate for society more inclusive concepts of what "love" and "family" mean.

We also continue to be at the forefront of the fight for justice and equality for all people. From Baynard Rustin marching for civil rights with Martin Luther King, Jr. in the 1960's, to Audre Lorde and the feminist movement of the 1970's, to Harvey Milk, Cleve Jones, and Larry Kramer, gay people have been leaders at rallying people together in ensuring equal rights for everyone.

Throughout our struggles, we, as a community, have maintained our inner child. We know how to be playful and have fun. We're not worried about making fools out of ourselves, and this extreme freedom and playfulness has great healing power for our world. Many straight people remark how it's their gay friends with whom they have the most fun.

Ellen DeGeneres is a great example of someone who uses her gay gift of playfulness to help uplift the spirits of her mostly straight female talk-show audience. Her humor is never mean-spirited, and her silly dancing, skits and mono-logues are wonderful expressions of how our gay giftedness can enliven and enlighten the world through our joyfulness and liveliness. Henri Nouwen had this childlike enthusiasm, too.

Spiritual teachers throughout time have stressed the importance of being like little children. When asked who is the greatest in the kingdom of heaven (or, metaphysically, who is closest to enlightenment and peace), Jesus pointed to a little child and said, "Unless you become as little children, you will by no means enter the kingdom of heaven."

It is our childlike playfulness that gets us in touch with our spirit. When those around us witness this, they, in turn, feel comfortable enough to express their own magnificence. We open the gate to the world of Spirit.

The use of our gay gift has helped heterosexual women be more sexually free, has made heterosexual men become more nurturing and sensitive, and has enabled those around us to become more playful and expressive.

In the quote that begins this section and in her book *The Spirit of Intimacy,* Sobonfu Somé writes that gay people are spiritual gatekeepers. Our gift can help open the gate for others, showing them the entrance to the spiritual world. We are gatekeepers between the physical world and the world of the Divine.

The Dagara tribe in Africa believes that gay people are the guardians of the doorways into other worlds or realities, and that much of the pain in the world can be traced to the disrespect given to these spiritual gatekeepers.

The Dagara tribe believes that our world is not only physical, but possesses other energetic realities that are crucial to the spiritual health of each person in the community. The gatekeeper, who is born with special gifts of connection, facilitates the entrance to this spiritual world. "All gays and lesbians are gatekeepers," said Somé. "Without the gatekeeper, we're left with a gate unattended."

So, when our religious leaders today denounce homosexuality and exclude gay people from their churches, they are, in actuality, leaving the gate to the spiritual world unattended. In their attempts to keep us from our giftedness, these so-called religious leaders are, in fact, harming their congregants and their communities.

Christian de la Huerta, author of *Coming Out Spiritually*, says that being gay is a spiritual calling and that gay people "are the spiritual warriors, the scouts of consciousness who are integrating spirit and sexuality for much of the rest of society. We owe these modern-day shamans the latitude they need and the respect they deserve to do this crucial work."

"It is a great skill - one pleasing to 'God,' I think - to be able to rise above your religious opinions and see through to something higher and more subtle (this is what the Buddhists call Enlightenment). It is a 'gift from God' that gay people get to be skilled at this."

- Toby Johnson

<u>The Gift of Light</u>

A Light Worker is an individual who dedicates his/her life to the cultivation of inner presence and the elevation of awareness in self and in others.

Like Eckhart Tolle writes, gay people have an advantage when it comes to Enlightenment (meaning "In the Light") simply by coming out of the closet and embracing their true inner Spirit. Once we have done so, our role is to help others achieve Enlightenment.

The Gay Lightworkers website states: "Lightworkers are people on earth at this time whose purpose involves raising the consciousness of the planet in some way. For some this can be teaching, for others it can be by spreading joy and laughter, or for others it might even be tearing down the old way of doing things. As gay people, we possess all of these things. However, what is most important is that we contain both male and female aspects of ourselves. This gives gay people an awareness of what the Spirit really is."

Which brings us back to the Native American "Two Spirits," who were revered as holy (whole-y) beings, because they embodied a balance between the male and the female, bringing them closer to the true nature of the Spirit.

Now, I know some gay men today who will defensively state, "There is nothing feminine about me!" as a way to combat the gay stereotype out there equating this with weakness. To that I say, the feminine side of you is not your weakness, but your strength. Learn to embrace it, and you'll help to heal the world.

Think about it: the places around the world that most oppress women and gay people are often the ones in crisis and conflict and poverty. These are often the places in most need of healing.

Despite this fact, many gay men still reject their feminine side as something they need to eradicate or bury under lots of packing peanuts, keeping their giftedness at bay. I, too, have been there. I came out during the height of the AIDS crisis, when being gay was also viewed as being weak. In response, we bulked up our bodies at the gym and took to the streets wearing combat boots and military jackets.

Some gay men even took out personal ads stating that they were "straight acting and appearing" and seeking only the same in a partner, adding *"No femmes"* to the list of qualities they most sought in a potential mate.

We ran from the feminine, and, understandably, we also ran from religion, as it was within the very walls of the churches, temples and synagogues of our youths where we heard the most unloving things about our very natures. Some of the biggest damage inflicted on our psyches and our souls have come from these supposedly sacred places.

Sadly, however, we threw the baby out with the bathwater. When we ran from religion, many of us also ran from the Spirit, as somehow we equated spirituality with organized religion. In doing so, many of us lost touch with our giftedness as Whole-y men and women. We lost touch with our gift of Light.

You've heard the term *flamer* to refer negatively to gay men? Well, let's embrace that term, as we have with *queer*. We are *flamers* in the best sense, as we're like the lamp lighters of yore, who kept the street lamps lit at night so that people could find their way home.

Our Gay Gift of Light can help others find their way home, too - home being the True Self inside. However, before we can begin to help heal the world, we must get back in touch with our own giftedness.

Many of us have lost touch with it by caring more for ourselves than for others. By failing to embrace our gay elders. By ignoring those whom our gay community deems "unattractive." By partaking in gossip instead of kindness. By placing too much emphasis on body and mind, and too little on spirit. By listening to the messages of the world, rather than the voice inside.

Your light may be dim, but it's still there, just waiting for you to turn up the flame. The world is depending on it.

As Toby Johnson writes in his groundbreaking book *Gay Perspective*, "In mythic and metaphysical terms, (gay people) are more likely to see the universe the way God sees it, freed from the blinders of duality and polarization. The effort to see beyond duality is the aim of most religious and mystical traditions; it is specifically identified as the foundation of the yogic traditions of Hinduism and Buddhism. Most of us gay people, as a side-effect of our sexuality abnormality, are bestowed by the universe with this gift of insight. The trick for us, of course, is to recognize and embrace the gift."

"What we think, we become. All that we are arises with our thoughts. With our thoughts, we make the world."

- Buddha

<u>Popping the Bubble Wrap</u>

Visualization is a great tool for helping you reconnect with your Spirit. Readers of the popular book *The Secret* or those who've studied the Law of Attraction may be familiar with the use of Treasure Maps or Vision Boards.

For example, I created the cover for this book before I even wrote it, and I placed the cover on my Vision Board, which is a bulletin board I keep above my desk where I do my writing. Around the cover, I placed words I had cut out of magazines. One phrase says, *"To Teach Others What We Know"* and another, *"Helping Others Gives Our Lives True Meaning."*

Words and images are also energy and are, therefore, extremely powerful. Japanese researcher Masaru Emoto recently experimented with words and water. When he and his colleagues affixed words like *"Hitler"* or *"I'm Going to Kill You"* on glass water jars and then froze them, the ice crystals that formed were dark, unhealthy, and hideously misshapen, but when they taped words like *"Mother Teresa"* and *"Love"* on them, the crystals formed were luminous: bright, beautifully shaped and brilliantly spectacular.

The same held true when he and his colleagues played certain types of music or sent out thoughts to the glass jars. The photographic evidence of his work can be found in his book *The Message From Water*.

Dr. Emoto's work clearly demonstrates that our words and our thoughts have a profound effect on our bodies (which are mostly made of water) and our world (again, mostly water). We can positively heal and transform ourselves and our planet by the thoughts we choose to think.

So, I want you to visualize your gay gift and send loving thoughts its way. I not only want you to picture this in your head, but I want you to literally create this visual. You will need a medium-sized gift box, a Sharpie marker, gift-wrapping supplies like a nametag, packing peanuts and bubble wrap, plus a medium-sized rock for this exercise.

Your rock should be big enough for you to write *"Gay is a Gift"* on it with a Sharpie. Or maybe you prefer writing *"Light Worker"* or *"Two Spirit"* or *"Rainbow Child"* on the rock instead. Pick a phrase which best represents your gay giftedness to you.

Next, wrap the rock with some bubble wrap (preferably, use the sheets which have the bigger size bubbles, as you'll be writing on these, too) and place it inside the box. Finally, fill the box with packing peanuts and then put the cover on the box and affix a gift tag to it. Address the tag to yourself (*"To: Salvatore,"* for example) and then write that the gift is *"From: Spirit,"* or whichever term feels most comfortable for you, such as *"From: the Living Light,"* *"From: Divine Wisdom,"* or *"From: God."* (I actually prefer for the gift tag to be signed *"Love:"* instead of *"From:"* for this gift has been given to you with love).

Finally, place the gift box on your desk, on a bathroom shelf, on the kitchen counter, on your bedroom nightstand, or wherever you will see it most throughout the day. Every time you look at it, you will be reminded of your gay giftedness, and I want you to then send good and positive thoughts its way. This visualization is very powerful, but to fully activate it, you must begin to dig through the packing peanuts and start popping the bubble wrap. Let me explain.

Maybe you've buried your gay gift for many years under mountains of packing peanuts in your attempts to keep it hidden from view, so now you'll have to dig to get at it, but, don't worry: your gift is still there just waiting to be found and put to good use. Think of the anticipation you'll feel as you dig, find, and reveal your gift to the world. It's a gift to pass on to others, a gift of Light to share with the world.

As for the bubble wrap, it serves a purpose, too, to protect your precious gift ("A living stone rejected by men, but approved and *precious* in God's sight," says Scripture) but, guess what? It's something you don't need for your gift. Why is that? Because, though your gift may be precious, it is also rock solid! It cannot be damaged or destroyed. The bubble wrap is only getting in the way of revealing your gift to the world.

And, yet, so many of us keep our gift hidden under layers of bubble wrap, each bubble representing a different negative thought which we think we need in order to protect ourselves, when, in actuality, they're smothering our gift and not giving it a chance to breathe. (Which reminds me that the Latin word for '*breathe*' is '*Spiritus.*' Our Spirits need to breathe!).

What are some of those negative thoughts smothering our gift? They're thoughts of fear, anxiety, resentment. They're the things our ego tells us in order to keep us from reconnecting with our Spirit. You see, once you start reconnecting with your Gift, your ego no longer serves a purpose, so it will do anything to stay alive, such as feed your mind with negative and self-defeating thoughts.

I used to think that ego was a term that didn't apply to me. I reserved this word for the self-absorbed beauty queen, the Wall Street mogul, or the blinged out rapper. As I've grown in consciousness, I've come to understand that ego is the incessant "monkey mind" chatter in our head that keeps our focus away from the Present moment, which is where our Spirit lives.   I like how Dr. Wayne Dyer refers to ego as standing for *E*dging *G*od *O*ut, for it truly does keep us from reconnecting with our Spirit.

You may wonder why I use the term *"reconnecting"* rather than *"connecting."*   It's because we come from Spirit. We *are* Spirit, so we can never really be disconnected.   It's just that we've forgotten that we are Light.

Think of it as a pilot light.   The Light has always been on inside you, but you've forgotten to turn it up, so to speak. The ego wants you to keep your pilot light dim, because once you increase the intensity of the flame, the ego will be burned away.

Controlling those negative thoughts is one of the most difficult tasks, but it's imperative to do so in order to release the true brilliance of your Gift of Light.

John J. McNeill has been a hero to the gay Catholic community for decades. A Jesuit priest for 40 years, McNeill was forced by the Vatican to leave the priesthood if he continued to minister to the gay and lesbian community. McNeill left religious life with no bank account, health insurance, etc., but he did not abandon his faith nor his dedication to serving the gay community.

McNeill writes in his book *Sex As God Intended*, "Each of us have direct access to the knowledge of God's will for us through the Spirit dwelling in our hearts...If we place an action in harmony with the indwelling Spirit, we will experience deep peace and joy. On the contrary, if we place action that separates us from the indwelling Spirit, we will know anxiety and depression."

Have you ever heard the story of the "Two Wolves"? It's an old Cherokee story, in which a tribal leader tells his grandson about the battle which goes on inside of all people.

"My son, the battle is between two wolves inside us

40

all," the old Cherokee said. "One represents anger, jealousy, sorrow, envy, regret, arrogance, greed, self-pity, ego, false pride, superiority, anxiety, guilt, and inferiority.

"The other wolf represents peace, joy, serenity, humility, kindness, compassion, empathy, hope, truth, love and generosity."

The grandson thought about this for a few minutes, and then asked his grandfather, "So, which wolf wins the battle?"

The old Cherokee replied, "The one you feed."

Feeding the second wolf instead of the first one takes lots of practice, but please don't let that discourage you from commencing on what you'll find is a life-changing (and a life-giving) exercise.

The key is to stay in the *present.* This should be easy to remember, since you're looking at a gift box which contains your Spiritual *present.* Looking at this present each day is a great reminder to remain in the present...and to remember your Spiritual presence, too!

Why does staying in the present help you to control your negative thoughts? Well, think about it: most negative thoughts we tell ourselves are either about things that happened in the past or things that may happen in the future.

Since the past is over and the future doesn't yet exist, all you have is the Now moment. This is why Eckhart Tolle entitled his book *The Power of Now*, but this is a wisdom handed down to us from all the great Way Showers, one of whom, Buddha, wrote "The secret of health for both mind and body is not to mourn for the past or worry about the future, but to live in the present moment."

And, in a book translated as *Abandonment to the Present Moment* (or *Abandonment to Divine Providence*), a French Jesuit priest named Jean Pierre de Caussade wrote, "The secret is focusing upon the present moment," and he wrote this more than three hundred years before Eckhart Tolle and *The Secret.*

As I stated in the introduction to this book, this wisdom has been with us through the ages - the same lesson taught to us over and over again by a multitude of spiritual men and women from diversely different backgrounds. So, why is this message still not getting through to us? Why is it so difficult to apply this key teaching to our lives?

Try this the next time a negative thought comes into your mind: Pop it! You can do this figuratively in your mind, of course, but I'd encourage you do it literally, too. Visualization is powerful, right?

Go back to that bubble wrap in your gift box (your present, remember?) and write your negative thought on a bubble (that's why I mentioned getting the big ones) using a Sharpie marker. You may not have enough room to write out the whole thought, but even just a word or two (like "Fear" or "Lack") will do the trick.

Next comes the fun part: Go ahead and pop that thought! Literally. Stand up with the bubble wrap in hand and announce aloud, "I am popping this thought now and forever!" Pop! Let the noise snap you back into the present moment. Then affirm aloud the opposite of that thought. For example, if your negative thought concerns lack, speak thoughts of abundance.

Now that we've begun popping the bubbles, we can focus on uncovering our G.I.F.T.

"Homosexuality is indeed a remarkable gift. Gay people are a gift to the community, bringing particular qualities and insights, not in spite of, but because of, their gayness."
　　　　　　　　　　　　- Roman Catholic priest, Maurice Shinnick

G.I.F.T.

How do we begin to get back in touch with the gay giftedness we may have initially rejected, kept hidden or failed to bring to fruition due to the negative thoughts we've told ourselves? It's there underneath all those packing peanuts and bubble wrap, but now we need to get to it.

Controlling our "monkey mind" chatter and staying in the present moment is not easy, but if you take to heart the following acronym I've devised for the word "gift" and apply it to your life each and every day, I promise it will get easier, and you will find yourself more and more at peace.

Just remember that the acronym for your G.I.F.T. stands for :

Gratitude
Inspiration
Forgiveness
Trust

Let's take them one at a time.

G

"For everything that has been, I say thank you, and to all that will be, I say yes."   -Dag Hammarskjold

GRATITUDE:

The first step is gratitude, which is easy to remember since the first thing most of us do when we receive a gift is say, "Thank you."

Being grateful for the many blessings the Universe has bestowed on us is one of the quickest ways to put us on the vibration of peacefulness and abundance.

When we focus on the past or the future, we are sending out thoughts of lack, and by the Law of Attraction, we will, therefore, receive more thoughts of lack.

"If only..." thoughts, such as *"If only I had picked a different career path..."* or *"If only I had chosen a different partner..."* put our focus on the past.

Consequently, *"When I..."* thoughts, such as *"When I find the right job..."* or *"When I meet the right person..."* put our focus on the future.

Our focus needs to be on the present moment, and gratitude not only helps us to do this, but it brings more things to be grateful for into our lives.

One of the best ways to maintain an "attitude of gratitude" is to keep a gratitude journal. This is so easy to do, yet the rewards it brings are enormous.

First, gift yourself with a nice blank journal. You certainly can use a cheap spiral notebook or yellow legal pad, but I recommend finding a more special and substantial tome to record and honor your blessings.

Your neighborhood bookstore (and, if you have a gay bookstore near your house, *definitely* patronize them) is filled with dozens of different types of journals from rich leather bound ones to brightly-colored hard covered ones with various designs on them. It's okay to splurge a little here, for this is one of the best gifts you can give yourself.

Once you have your special journal, find a quiet time and place to sit for just a few moments each day and simply reflect on at least five things for which you are grateful that day.

Some people keep their gratitude journals on their nightstands, and use the time before bed to do this. It's a good way to reflect upon the events of the day, plus it puts you on a vibration of gratitude right before you go to sleep.

Sleep not only rejuvenates our bodies, but our spirits, as well, and dreams are messengers of creativity, so putting yourself on the wavelength of gratitude right before you drift off to sleep can be extremely beneficial.

That said, it's important to remember not to focus on the *could-a, would-a, should-a*'s of the day's events, such as "*I should have done this...*" or "*I could have done that...,*" but, rather, keep your focus only on the things that happened that day for which you are grateful.

I am usually very tired by day's end, so I choose to write in my gratitude journal in the morning after I finish my meditation (which I'll discuss later in the "Inspiration" chapter). Writing in my gratitude journal only takes five minutes, and I find it really helps me set the tone for the day. I simply think back on the past twenty-four hours, and I jot down all the things that happened for which I am grateful.

Again, I'm not thinking back on things I could have done differently or things I failed to accomplish. Rather, I start off my day with thoughts of gratitude, so the Universe responds in-kind throughout my day providing me with more and more things for which to be grateful.

If you have difficulty with either of these times, then simply find any five quiet minutes of the day (free of distraction, of course) to record in your journal, maybe in the middle of your day during your lunch hour or on the train ride to or from work.

This exercise seems so simple to do - and it is - yet it's one of the most powerful tools to connect us with our inner gay giftedness. Put this into practice each day, and you will begin to transform.

All of a sudden, you'll find yourself actively on the lookout for things to be thankful for throughout your day. You'll start noticing everything. You will be "in the moment," as they say. You will find yourself truly present, not thinking about the past or the future, but simply enjoying the moment at hand (for "the queen/kingdom of God is *at hand,*" or in the present).

When first starting this exercise, however, you may struggle to come up with even five things to write down. Be patient with yourself. Remember, there's always something for which to be thankful.

It doesn't need to be something big. It could be something as simple as a smile from a stranger, a coin found on the floor, or free address labels in the day's mail. Though these things may seem small, by acknowledging and blessing them, we see their greatness.

Biting into a juicy apple, I silently give thanks for the tree which provided this nourishment for me and for the farmers and truckers and grocers, too, who helped bring it to my table.

Hearing my cat silently purring next to me, I tell him, "Thank you for coming into my life and gifting me with your spirit."

Finding my favorite box of cereal on sale for two dollars, and then having a dollar coupon to use on it as well, I give thanks for the good fortune that's come my way.

"Thank you" is a prayer, and it's one of the best I know. Prayer is simply remembering your Spirit, and one of the ways we can realign ourselves with our Source is by sustaining an attitude of gratitude throughout the day even when - *especially* when - things appear stressful.

Take a few moments to do so right now. Space is provided here, or you can use a gratitude journal if you already have one.

Today's date:_____

THANK YOU for...

1._____

2._____

3. _____

4. _____

5. _____

... now HOW MAY I SERVE?

Notice how I end my entry with a response to the Source that has brought me so much abundance: How may I serve you?

When someone presents you with a gift, they are letting you know how much you are appreciated. In a way, their present is a way of saying thanks for your presence. Your "thank you" in return for the gift is a prayer not only to the giver, but to the Giver of all good things.

I encourage you to say "Thank You" throughout your day to the birds, the trees, the comfortable chair you're sitting in, the great meal you're eating, or the inspiring music to which you're listening.   Each one of our senses (we're "sensitive," remember?) gets us in touch with lots for which to be thankful.

Of course, if you're, say, standing on a subway platform alone, thankful for the warm cup of coffee you're drinking, you may be hesitant to shout "Thank You!" out loud, so, in cases like this, you may want to just say it quietly to yourself, maybe just a whispered "Thanks" to the Universe. But, if you're in a place where you can freely shout, I encourage you to shout!   Remember, there's inherent power in your words and your thoughts.

Before moving on to the next section, take some time here (or in your gratitude journal) to reflect on how thankful you are to be gay. Though our childhoods, adolescences and coming out experiences may have been painful ones, think about the many gifts that have come from those experiences. These gifts have made us more compassionate, less judgmental; more expressive, less afraid; and more gentle, less rigid.

Use this prompt to start:

Divine Spirit Within Me,
I am grateful for the gift of being gay, as it has better enabled me to:

_____

_____

_____

_____

_____

I

"Meditation means to be constantly extricating yourself from the clinging of the mind. Inspiration is God making contact with Itself."
                                        - Ram Dass

<u>INSPIRATION</u>

Let's say there's someone you'd like to know better. Well, you could Google his/her name and try to find out some information about them that way, or you could talk to some of his/her friends and learn some more. There's a lot of valuable information you can learn about a person this way.

But the best way to know this person better, of course, is to spend lots of time with him/her. One-on-one alone time.

It seems quite obvious, yet this is not always true of some (but not all) of the "religious" people I've encountered over the years and their own relationship with Jesus/God/Spirit. Sure, they've taken part in Bible studies and can quote Scripture backwards and forwards. They're in church every Sunday and faithfully listen to preachers talk about and discuss Jesus/God/Spirit (Body/Mind/Soul).

Yet, I've come to find that some of these very people do not actually spend alone time with Jesus or God or Spirit each day. They may know God on an intellectual level, but the only true way to *really* know the Divine is by devoting ourselves to quiet time alone in its presence each and every day.

Malcolm Boyd (an Episcopal priest who came out of the closet in 1977, becoming the most prominent gay clergy member in America at the time) refers to this type of worship as "Churchianity," which he explains "is conventional church-going without a prophetic quality or a hint of mysticism."

As Thomas E. Powers writes in his book *First Questions on the Life of the Spirit*, these people may be spiritually awake, but they are not spiritually alive.

And I don't mean to just single out those who are involved in organized religion. There are also many New Age spiritual seekers I've met who have read every New Thought book, attended hundreds of conferences, and, in doing so, have attained an intellectual understanding of the workings of the Spirit.

Yet it never goes any further for them, because they fail to spend time alone in meditation and prayer each day. There is no other way for you to truly reconnect with your Giftedness without this daily discipline.

Now, I know some of you may bristle at hearing words like "prayer" and "discipline," but what I'm talking about is simply quieting yourself for at least a half-hour each day, removing all distractions, and spending time remembering your Spirit, remembering your Gift. When we do this, we are "in Spirit," and inspiration takes place.

"You don't have the time for that" may be one of ego's negative thoughts to get you from spending time with its enemy, the Spirit. Pop the bubble on thoughts like this, and make the time each day for meditation and prayer.

Do not be intimidated by these words. Meditation doesn't mean that you have to sit on the floor like an Indian guru repeating some ancient chant (though some may find that helpful, at times), and prayer doesn't mean that you have to say set prayers you memorized as a child (though some may find that helpful, at times).

Malcolm Boyd describes prayer this way, "To pray is to be silently present with God. To be deeply grateful. To ask for nothing at all. To offer. To be content with emptiness. To look at the entire cosmos as if it were a small leaf or bud. To walk on a city street or in nature. To make love. To make music. To sit beneath a tree. To eat hot soup and warm bread. By my definition, prayer is consciously hanging out with God; being with God in a deliberate way."

I love that: being with God in a deliberate way. Taking apart the word "deliberate," I see it as "de-*liberate*" or "of liberation." When we pray, we are free! Free of the "monkey mind" chatter, we set our Spirits free.

Maybe it would be less intimidating for some of you if I shared with you my daily practice. Each morning, I get up at 5:30 am, while it's still pitch dark and very quiet outside, and I walk into a small sitting room on the side of my house where there's a high-backed chair and an old trunk which serves as a coffee table.

Before taking my seat in the chair, I light a candle which sits atop the trunk, as this candle will be a focal point for my meditation and will remind me of the Light within me and within every living thing.

Sitting upright in the chair, I place my arms at my sides with my palms up, a gesture that I'm ready to receive the Light of the Spirit, and also to give it back out into the world.

And then I just sit in quiet. Of course, distractions come into my head at times (worries about the day's events or feelings of inadequacies, for example), but I let these go. How? Well, sometimes I'll repeat a simple affirmation like "*Peace. Be Still.*" I say this silently in my head or whisper it aloud.

The mantra of these words brings me back to the present Now moment where I can be still, sit in silence, focus on my breathing, and remember that the Divine is within me.

Visualization also helps here, too. The great mystic, Teresa of Avila, meditated by visualizing going from her home (earthly existence) into a castle (home of the Spirit). As she crossed the moat and entered the castle, she'd visualize the drawbridge closing, so she'd be alone with the Spirit.

I sometimes visualize walking alone along a beach near my home and finding a secret alcove among the rocks which dot the shoreline. In this alcove or cave, it is dark and I am alone, but I am not afraid. It is here where I wait for the Spirit to speak to me.

What I am listening for is my inner voice, the voice of the Divine within, which reminds me of who I really am and what it is I've come here to accomplish. It reminds me of my interconnectedness with all people and with all life.

Often, I am moved to tears by its revelations - things I have always known about myself, but had forgotten. It also reminds me of my special gay giftedness and the divine purpose for my life.

I finish my meditation with prayer, which, for me, is sending a simple, yet powerful "Thank You" for Divine wisdom and guidance, and then I send out my Light, my positive thoughts and energies, to those people for whom I'm remembering in special way that day. They may be a friend or family member in ill health, a colleague celebrating a birthday, or a prayer for a stranger who might be hurting. Again, I let Spirit guide my prayer.

Finally, I wiggle my fingers and toes and slowly come back into my physical body, ready to greet the day at hand. Sometimes, I recite the prayer of Mychal Judge, the gay Catholic priest who died in the collapse of the World Trade Center on September 11. Mychal began his days with the prayer, *"Spirit, take me where you want me to go this day. Let me meet the people you want me to meet. Tell me what to say, and keep me out of your way."*

Mychal, by the way, knew that "Gay is a Gift" years before Rev. Ed Bacon spoke those words on Oprah. In his biography of Mychal Judge, the writer Michael Ford recounts how Mychal gradually "moved to a place of recognizing that being gay was a gift as opposed to a burden, wound or handicap - a gift of God and a gift of himself."

In the same book, Ford quotes gay activist Brendan Fay's take on his friend Mychal's thoughts on gay as a gift. Fay said, "Mychal would speak about acceptance and gift.

Never did I hear him speak about being gay as being a burden or a cross. He would say, 'It's wonderful, wonderful, wonderful. Look at who we are as gay people at this moment in history, as being a gift for the church, to witness change and be agents for change both within church and society.'"

I was fortunate enough to have worked with Mychal Judge during my years as a religious brother in the Catholic Church, and his image is one of the icons I sometimes place next to the candle during my morning meditation. I have often felt his Spirit and guidance during those moments of silence.

While prayer and mediation are key aspects of the spiritual life, it's important to find other ways of connecting with the Spirit, too. What do you do to get inspired or in Spirit?

Think about the things that have inspired you in the past. Maybe you attended a play or a concert, watched a Special Olympian compete, or gazed at a beautiful sunset and remarked, "This is inspiring!" That's because something in your Spirit connected with the Spirits of the artists, the athlete or the sky.

Like many, I connect with the Spirit when I'm alone in nature. Ralph Waldo Emerson wrote of his nature walks, "In the woods, we return to reason and faith. There I feel that nothing can befall me in life - no disgrace, no calamity (leaving me my eyes), which nature cannot repair. Standing on the bare ground - my head bathed by the blithe air and uplifted into infinite space - all mean egotism vanishes. I become a transparent eye-ball; I am nothing! I see all; the currents of the Universal Being circulate through me; I am part or parcel of God."

So, go for a hike, sit under a shade tree, write a poem, read about an inspirational life, or listen to a beautiful piece of music. (Music *really* inspires me, and is part of my daily meditation practice. See the appendix of this book for some of my favorite CD selections). Do whatever it takes so you can get to know the Spirit better.

And, remember the words of Ram Dass which head up this section. Ram Dass is a gay man and world-renowned spiritual guru, who has been a mentor to Dr. Wayne Dyer and many other contemporary spiritual writers and teachers. I urge you to pick up one of his books (see reference section in the appendix of this book), but, for now, I will close this section with some of his wisdom:

"Indians live as if they are souls and Americans live as if they are egos....Spiritual practices like meditation help us move from identifying with the ego to identifying with the soul...It is important to expect nothing, to take every experience, including the negative ones, as merely steps on the path, and to proceed."

Before you move on, take some time here (or in your gratitude journal) to reflect on the things that inspire you and then consider how your being gay informs them.

Here's your prompt: *I am most In-Spirit, most in touch with my Gay Gift, when I'm....*

_____

_____

_____

_____

_____

_____

Before we venture on to step three, I'd like to share a bit of my own beginnings with incorporating steps one and two into my own life. I hope these words will give you some encouragement for your own journey.

I had been writing in my gratitude journal each day, and making meditation and prayer part of my daily routine for about three months' time, but I still couldn't stop the negative thoughts swirling around in my head, impeding my progress.

I was on a Mediterranean cruise with my partner - our first real vacation in years - but I was not at peace. Here's what I wrote in a journal at that time:

"Sailing on the Mediterranean Sea, I think of Odysseus. Whenever I taught Homer's *The Odyssey* to my high school freshmen classes, I always enjoyed talking with my students about the importance of Odysseus finding his way home.

"As I've grown in consciousness recently, I've begun to rethink Odysseus's connection to home. I'm thinking maybe Homer was writing about our inner home, our being, and that Odysseus's quest was from ego (tempted by the Circe and the Sirens; battles with the sea and the wind) to finding his true home: Peace.

"Although I'm 'getting it' (meaning that my Spirit has been responding and the Universe is speaking), I still struggle with negativity. I read yesterday about *deliberate* creation, and I focused on the word. I saw that 'liberate' was part of the word, and I see that I must make a conscious effort to deliberately direct my thoughts to the positive, if I'm going to ever be free. It is a discipline, I know, which reminds me that I'm a disciple. I know that by setting out upon this path, my ego is fighting to survive, hence my battles with negativity. I'm not really sure what to do, but I remain open and receptive to Spirit."

If you're experiencing what I did, don't despair. Like with diet and exercise, the results may not be seen right away, but they *are* taking effect. Trust me on this. You can't learn to play a musical instrument in one day. It takes practice, practice, practice. The same is true for the spiritual life.

"Take the first step in faith. You don't have to see the whole staircase, just take the first step," said Martin Luther King.

It's important to remember this as we venture into step three, Forgiveness, which often requires the most patience.

F

"There is really nothing difficult about letting this inner light shine. All we must do is correct the tendency to turn off this light when we face darkness." - Eric Butterworth

FORGIVENESS:

I find that this step is the most difficult for gay people, as we have a lot of hurt to overcome.

Many of us still have a tough time forgiving our families, friends, teachers, ministers and society in general for their failure to embrace us when we came out.

Many of us still harbor old grudges against the childhood bullies who taunted us for being different, and present day grudges against our government for failing to recognize us as full and equal citizens.

And some of us hold grudges against our own gay community for failing to accept us for not living up to our culture's standards of beauty.

There's a lot of hurt we hold inside, and some may argue that our response to it is justified, for we have been wronged. Yes, our churches did us wrong. Yes, our government did us wrong. Yes, the bullies who made our childhoods hell did us wrong.

But now it's time to let it go. For good. For God. For Give.

Remember the wisdom we've been given about letting go of the past and staying in the present? Well, we need to apply it again here in step three.

Again, the ego will fight you tooth-and-nail on this. *"Remember, when you came out to your parents, and your father told you that you were going to rot in Hell?"* your ego reminds you. *"How can you forgive something like that?"*

But you must. It happened in the past, and the secret is staying in the present Now moment. Like with your negative thoughts in step two, your ego here doesn't want you to forgive, for if you do, you will no longer have any need of it and it will die. Remember, you will never be at peace if you don't learn to forgive, and peacefulness is what sets our gay gift free.

Charles Fillmore, the cofounder of the Unity, wrote, "Life can be unfair, cruelties and hurts happen, and justice does not always prevail...It is so easy to internalize those hurts until they become deep-seated resentments that hamper and limit us...There is a better way. It is in loosening the bonds of old and unproductive ways of thinking and setting ourselves free. Remember, the other person does not have to change for us to be free. We have to change...We have the ability to set ourselves free through the activity of the mind."

Now, too, we must forgive the resentment we hold against political and religious institutions. Forgiveness doesn't mean excusing or allowing injustice. We, of course, need to raise awareness and work for equality. What forgiveness does is in some ways more for the forgiver than the forgivee.

I was recently grocery shopping with a friend, and she refused to buy a certain brand of eggs, because the cartons had the Christian fish symbol and Biblical quotes on them.

"I refuse to support them," she said defiantly. I couldn't really argue with her, as I have in the past decided not to use the services of a real estate agent who also had the Christian fish symbol on his business card.

On the other hand, I'd be furious about someone who refused to patronize a store which displayed the gay pride rainbow sticker on their window.

Many Christian churches have let us know they don't want us, and many in the gay community have let them know we don't want them, and all of this exclusion has created an "us" versus "them" mentality, which keeps us all from remembering that we are all of the One Spirit.

Then, of course, many gay people have had tortuous childhoods, being taunted with words like "sissy" and "faggot." Then there are those of us who have had horrendous things happen to us in our lives, things we think we cannot possible get over or forgive.

Mark Anthony Lord, a gay man and founder of the Bodhi Spiritual Center in Chicago, has written (in "Science of Mind" magazine) of a painful time in his life when he couldn't seem to make amends with his past and life's hurts.

Talking with his spiritual advisor, Lord asked her what he could possibly do to get over this pain.

"Through my tears," he writes, "I told her of my tortured childhood, of sexual abuse and being called a 'sissy,' 'faggot,' and all the other names kids use against gay boys. I told her how as a young man, I slept with more people than I could count to cover the pain and the shame. My promiscuity ruined my relationships and nearly destroyed my career and many friendships. I asked her what I could do to stop this pain."

Lord's spiritual practitioner paused for a long time and then said, "Forgive. You have to forgive yourself and everyone who ever did anything to you. Forgiveness will set you free."

Jesus also had a similar message about forgiveness, about turning the other cheek. I realize that some of you may have a negative connotation when you hear the name Jesus, because you still hold much resentment against the Christian churches which use the name of Jesus to teach fear and hatred.

But, whether you believe he was the Savior or not, Jesus was a great spiritual teacher and Way Shower who shared Divine wisdom with humanity, especially when it came to forgiveness.

Jesus, the man, had reached the highest state of Awareness, the Christ-consciousness. He taught us that we, too, had this Christ-consciousness, this same Spirit or Living Light, within us, and he gave us all the instructions we need for connecting with it. By practicing these teachings, we'd achieve even greater things than he did, he said.

So, what were his instructions about forgiveness? When Jesus was asked how many times we need to forgive those who have wronged us, he replied, "Seventy times seven times," reminding us that we need to keep forgiving over and over again.

And when he was dying on the cross, he exclaimed, "Father, forgive them, for they know not what they do." Jesus knew that those who had done this to him were not evil people, but were reacting based on their egos, their fears, and their limited ways of thinking.

His radical lifestyle and teachings were things that were fearful to the religious leaders of his time. He lived unconventionally, associated with the undesirables of society, and rebelled against the long-established religious rules. That's why they needed to silence him.

This reminds me a lot of the gay community, though I don't mean to imply that Jesus was gay. It is interesting to note, however, that a disproportionately large number of the most highly conscious spiritual teachers in the history of the world were men and women who refused to partner with the opposite sex.

If marriage and procreation are so sacred, then why did the majority of the most spiritually aware individuals on the planet refuse to partake in either?

In fact, the only place in the New Testament where Jesus really speaks of sexuality is in a discussion of eunuchs, a term many Biblical scholars today believe referred to gay people. When asked about the physical union between men and women, Jesus tells the disciples that some are not made for this, and are "born that way from their mother's womb."

In Jesus' time, eunuchs were well-respected for bein
teachers.

Though some scholars have argued that Jesus himse
lived as a eunuch, Malcolm Boyd refers to Jesus as queer,
"not in terms of sexual orientation but in life terms. He embraced diversity in startling ways, cutting against the grain of
social norms."

Many medieval mystics - both men and women - were
imprisoned, tortured or killed (sometimes by their own religious communities) for their own "cutting against the grain,"
for their unconventional behaviors and appearances and their
radical spiritual insights.

We still see the same today, like the recent split in the
Episcopal Church over the ordination of openly gay bishop
Gene Robinson. Jesus was inclusive, but, sadly, most Christian churches are not. Like many in the gay community, I can
get all riled up trying to defend my sexuality with religious
and political groups and organizations, but I know that this
"me" versus "them" mentality is not the answer towards
building bridges and fostering understanding.

As New Thought writer Eric Butterworth stated in the
quote which heads this section, we need to be careful not to
turn off our Light when we face darkness. We need to remember that our Light can heal these grudges and resentments
by love and by peace, not by friction and separation.

Henri Nouwen was a Catholic priest who wrote some
of the most simple, yet profoundly moving spiritual books of
the late twentieth century. He was also gay and a mystic. (In
fact, Nouwen often felt that the Evangelical Christians,
though word-centered and fervently committed, lacked the
mystical quality he felt was vital to spiritual living). Nouwen's words on forgiveness have been some of the most helpful to me on my spiritual journey.

He wrote, "Forgiveness is the name of love practiced
among people who love poorly. The hard truth is that all people love poorly. We need to forgive and be forgiven every

ncreasingly. That is the great work of love
ship of the weak that is the human family."

Ford, who wrote the biography on Father My-
also previously written a biography on Henri
ed *Wounded Prophet*, which I encourage you to
stingly enough, Ford's biography of Nouwen was
on My⌐ Judge's bedside nightstand at the time of his
death).

In *Wounded Prophet*, Ford reveals that Nouwen
planned to write a book about homosexuality and the Spirit,
but never did. I hope in some modest way that this book
you're now holding is a small step towards Nouwen's goal.

Here is another small taste of Nouwen's wisdom on
forgiveness for you to ponder, one which seems to hint at his
gay woundedness:

"Maybe the reason it seems hard for me to forgive others is that I do not fully believe that I am a forgiven person. If
I could fully accept the truth that I am forgiven and do not
have to live in guilt or shame, I would really be free. My freedom would allow me to forgive others seventy times seven
times. By not forgiving, I chain myself to a desire to get even,
thereby losing my freedom."

One of the ways you can free yourself from these
chains is another visualization technique. It's a "burning
bowl" ceremony.

After spending some quiet time in front of your meditation candle focusing on what you need to let go of in order
to be free, take a piece of paper and write down the name of a
person, an organization, or the particulars of a situation which
you need to forgive.

Bring your hurt, your burden, your resentment to the
Living Light candle, and let it a-Light your piece of paper.
(Of course, have a tin bucket, a small bowl of sand, or some
other receptacle at hand - you don't want to burn the house
down while you're doing this!).

As you watch the paper burn away, see it as a symbol

of your letting go of the situation. Affirm aloud or silently to yourself that you are free of the anger, the resentment, the grudge. For Good. For God. For Give.

I'll end this section with one of my favorite Buddhist stories:

Once there was a Buddhist monk who lived alone in a small hut at the bottom of a mountain. One night, when the monk was out, a thief broke into the hut and began to help himself to the monk's meager possessions.

The monk soon arrived and caught the thief stuffing things into a sack.

"You have come a long way to visit me," he said to the thief, "so you should not return empty-handed. Please take my clothes as a gift."

The monk then disrobed, stood naked in front of the thief, and handed over his clothes. The bewildered thief took the clothes and the other possessions and swiftly left the hut.

That night, the naked monk sat outside his hut and looked up at the full moon.

"Poor fellow," the monk said of the thief. "I wish I could give him this beautiful moon, too."

With love in his heart for the thief who took all his possessions, the monk slept peacefully under the stars.

Your prompt for this section is: *What I most need to let go of in order to more fully reconnect with my Gay Gift is....*

_____

_____

_____

_____

_____

_____

_____

_____

_____

I'm sometimes asked what it was that set me upon this Spiritual journey. Explaining that in its entirety would take up another whole book (one which I hope to write some day), but the short explanation is that I failed to embrace Trust.

During my years as a religious brother (and out gay man) in the Catholic Church, I believe I was becoming spiritually awake, but I was definitely not spiritually alive.

I am proud of the work I did during those years, teaching inner city youth and ministering to people with AIDS. I tried desperately during those years to be a bridge between the gay community and the church, until I realized that the celibate lifestyle was not life-giving for me.

Soon after leaving the Church, I met my partner, Gregg, and we would go on to open a successful bed-and-breakfast. Shortly after that, I signed my first book contract and was cast in a small role in a feature film. I had been hitting the gym religiously, too, and was in the best physical shape of my life.

A lot of good things were happening, but instead of bringing me peace, I found myself on the verge of a breakdown, though I now see it as a breakthrough.

Those worldly successes had fed my ego to the breaking point, to the point where I had forgotten my Spirit, though I didn't know it at the time. All I knew then was that none of my worldly accomplishments were bringing me peace. There was something missing. I wanted - I needed - to feel whole.

Then, one day, I noticed an ad in the classified section of the newspaper for which I write a column. It was seeking volunteers for a clinical drug trial. The upside was that it paid very well; the downside was that participants needed to live at the clinic (which was almost a two hour from my home) for an entire month, though there'd be a few sporadic days off here and there throughout the trial.

With the state my head was in at the time, the downside actually seemed desirable. I needed an escape from my world for awhile, plus, on those days off, I could stay with a friend, Jim (not his real name), who lived near the clinic.

Jim had parlayed his fame on a network reality show into a regular television gig, and I liked being seen around town with him when he was recognized, as if being seen in the company of a famous person somehow made me more important in people's eyes.

I was thrilled when I was accepted as one of the twelve participants in the drug trial. Arriving at the clinic to begin the study, all twelve of us had our suitcases searched, and we were required to pass through metal detectors. We were then shown to our dorm room and given medical scrubs to change into.

As we got to know one another over the coming days and weeks, it became clear that all twelve of us men were broken in some way. The majority of the participants (we affectionately called ourselves "lab rats") were unemployed, one was going through a painful divorce, another was about to have his home foreclosed on, and some were just hardened by life's circumstances.

In group situations like this, nicknames sometimes get applied, and I was christened "holy man" by the group, which was strange, since I hadn't discussed religion or spirituality with any of them. When I asked them why "holy man," one of the twelve said, "Because you're always so calm and peaceful and smiling all the time." Another, a young man who had recently been discharged from the military and with whom I had many heart to heart talks, suggested I become some sort of life coach.

During our time together in the clinic, the movie I had worked on - a legal thriller about a trial - was broadcast on cable television. As we watched it together one evening, none of the men made much of a fuss nor seemed very impressed by my brief appearance in the film. One even joked that if he had gone to the bathroom, he would have missed it.

The same was true when Jim's program came on television one day. "That's my friend," I proudly told the guys at the clinic, who, again, did not seem impressed. "Who is he?" inquired one with disinterest. My "fame," if you will, meant little to these men. They valued me as the "holy man."

One night at the clinic when I couldn't sleep, I prayed silently in bed, and a most blessed thing happened: Through the grace and insight of Spirit, I began to understand my gay giftedness. My gentleness, my openness, and my sensitivity were qualities that were valued by these men.

For years, my striving for success was driven by the rejection I felt growing up gay. I felt that if I could "make something of myself" - write a book, be in a movie - then I would prove to all those who made me feel "less than" that I was, indeed, somebody of worth.

The men at the clinic brought me to the realization that my worth was not in my worldly accomplishments, but in the bringing forth of the gift that was already inside me. Much like the outcome of a legal trial, I felt like I was "set free" by the end of that clinical trial. (And don't think I didn't see the symbolism of the twelve: twelve jurors, twelve apostles, twelve "lab rats").

When I returned home, I sought out a box of books I had in the basement from when I was in religious life. Sorting through it, I discovered one of my old journals that I had kept during my years as a monk.

As I picked it up, the journal seemed to open as if by

itself to a passage written in red ink, which was interesting to me, since I had kept the rest of the journal in either black or blue ink.

To this day, I have no idea why I wrote this passage in 1993, but there it was in my old journal. It was a quote from Saint John of the Cross. It said:

"I have abandoned all I ever sought to be, and in dying, my Spirit has been released."

As I read it, I fell to my knees and began sobbing on the floor of my basement. This was the big A-ha! moment I needed. This was the breakthrough.

I immediately realized that the peace I sought was only to be found in the abandonment of self. I needed to die to all my ego (or false self) ever sought to be, and start listening to what the *Spirit* (or True Self) wanted. *I* need to die, so that *Spirit* could live.

Though I grew up in the Catholic Church and had been a monk for six years of my adult life, I didn't really know much about the saints, nor did I consider them much, but after that A-ha!, I knew I needed to know more about John of the Cross.

I was afraid that most of the books I would find about this man would be overly pious accounts of his life, but among the list of books I was finding on Amazon, there was one whose cover spoke out to me. As I clicked on the author's name (Richard P. Hardy), I discovered that he had written another book entitled *Loving Men: Gay Partners, Spirituality and AIDS,* so I knew that his biography on John was the one I needed to read.

The more I learned about John from that book (edited by a nun named Sister *Salvatore*, of all things. My name!), the more astounded I was at our similarities: John came from a working class family and had two brothers (just like me). I learned that growing up, John, like me, was tender and gentle and more sensitive and thoughtful than other boys.

In his twenties, John volunteered his time working

with the sick and dying in hospitals (like I did with people with AIDS), and that he loved music and literature (my two passions). And, of course, we both entered religious orders in the Catholic Church.

When I got to the end of the book, I was floored by one more commonality: John died at midnight on December 13, which is my birthday. So, I knew this was *my* saint!

I now know that it was the Divine Grace of the Spirit which led me to discovering John of the Cross, whose life and example gave me the inspiration I needed to move forward spiritually.

What I learned from John of the Cross (not only from Hardy's biography, but from my own meditation experiences with John and his own writing, especially *Dark Night of the Soul*) is the basis for step four in uncovering our G.I.F.T.edness: Trust.

T

"Let the signs remind you we are passengers. Let the signs remind you to surrender."

- "Let Go, Let God" by Olivia Newton-John

TRUST

The ability to trust in the laws of the Universe, in the laws of Truth, means that one must be willing to surrender and put his/her Trust in Divine Providence.

Now, words like "surrender" and "abandonment" are hard ones for us to swallow, as they seem extremely defeatist, but they are vital ones for us to accept if we are serious about nurturing our gay gifts and our spiritual lives.

"Whoever seeks to follow me, must deny his very self," Jesus said, meaning that we must give up the ego's great need to control our lives if we seek to grow in consciousness.

This almost seems impossible for us in our modern age, as we are encouraged by our parents, our teachers and our culture to go after what we want and to make things happen for ourselves. We're told to be leaders, not followers.

The idea of simply being a passenger and just letting someone else do the driving - you've heard the term "Let Go, Let God" - seems foolish to us, but, in actuality, is following Divine Wisdom. Surrender and Trust seem to the ego like things of weakness, but in Truth, there is great strength in following the will of the Spirit.

People in twelve step programs know this better than most. The third step on the road to recovery is "We make the decision to turn our will over to the care of a Power greater than ourselves." Though we may not all be battling addictions to drugs or alcohol, many of us are addicted to the ego, and we need to surrender to the Spirit.

Strangely, this surrender doesn't feel like defeat. This is the "surrender that isn't surrender," which is spoken about in many religious texts. The reason it doesn't feel like defeat is because of the great freedom that is released in us when let go of the ego. As Scripture which says, *"It is in dying that we receive eternal life,"* meaning that when we give up the false self, we attain the true peacefulness of Spirit.

A modern adaptation of the Peace Prayer of St. Francis transforms the line *"It is in dying that we are born to eternal life"* to *"In living together in Oneness, we are truly born to eternal life."* Dying to self, then, really means finally coming to the realization that we are not separate from one another, but of the same Spirit. Only then will we experience true freedom.

Remember the frozen waffle commercial declaring, "Let go of my Eggo"? Well, your surrender is when you declare, "Let go of my Ego." It's not that you think less of yourself, it's that you think of yourself less.

This surrender is seen as vital to enlightenment in most spiritual traditions. In his book, *The Four Agreements*, Don Miguel Ruiz writes of the Mexican Toltec tradition and the "Imitation of the Dead," which encourages followers to be warriors against the parasite which had control of your mind. When we kill the parasite (the world's belief system, the ego), we "die" symbolically to Self.

When we die to ego, we grow in Spirit. We grow in awareness, as we let go of our selfish pursuits. The world we live in, however, is fixated on the Self. To be considered a success in the eyes of the world, one must draw attention to his/herself, accomplish certain things, amass the right material possessions, and fit the societal standards of beauty.

Most of us spend our lives in pursuit of whatever it takes to be considered successful in the eyes of the world, even if it means changing our appearance or buying things we don't really need.

Internet social networking sites like MySpace, Facebook and Twitter help us stay connected with one another, but, in some ways, the exploding popularity of those sites - and of reality television personalities, too - signals the desire many of us feel to bow to and prop up the ego's inherent need to be the star of the show.

Remember the Moby song, "We Are All Made of Stars?" Well, there's Truth to that. You *are* a star. We are all made of Light, made from the same Living Light. This is what illuminates us - the Light of the Spirit, not the spotlight of worldly recognition.

I'm reminded of a scene from the movie "Seven Years in Tibet," where Brad Pitt's character, Olympic hero Heinrich Harrer, is trying to impress a beautiful Tibetan woman by showing her his medals and newspaper clippings of his accomplishments. She responds something along the lines of: "That's the difference between the West and the East. You uphold and honor those who have built up their ego. We uphold and honor those who have torn down their ego."

Dying to self really means that you begin to see that your real "Self" is much bigger than just ego and the opinions other people hold about you.

In some ways, however, we as gay people have an advantage here, for, as Tolle says, in coming out of the closet and abandoning the world's expectations of what we *should* be, we surrender to the truth of the Spirit, the truth of who we really are. That's why coming out of the closet feels so freeing!. That said, we in the gay community can often times find ourselves trapped in a subculture that's extremely ego-focused, putting glamour, fame, material possessions, youth and beauty at the forefront.

Gay comic actor, Alec Mapa, jokes, "I belong to a gym, because I'm gay and live in L.A. and it's the law." Now, exercise is a wonderful thing, and it's important we take care of our bodies and our physical health.

It is through the body that we get to experience the world around us from the smell of the flowers to the sound of the birds, from the sight of a sunset to the touch of a loved one. We also use these bodies when we extend our gifts in service of others.

Many in our community, however, can sometimes take exercise to the extreme, more for the sake of vanity than for its health benefits. Walking, biking, hiking around nature and eating the right foods will keep you extremely healthy, but obsessing over the definition of your abdominal muscles has nothing to do with health, nor does building ridiculously enormous pectorals or biceps.

When we first came out of the closet, many of us experienced great freedom at no longer having to conform to familial and societal expectations of us, but then many of us felt like we needed to conform to the expectations of the gay community to which we were now a part.

This is why Eckhart Tolle says that, although we're at an advantage in terms of enlightenment, gay people can sometimes develop a sense of identity based on our gayness.

When that happens "you have escaped one trap," Tolle writes in *The Power of Now*, "only to fall into another. You will play roles and games dictated by a mental image you have of yourself as gay. You will become unconscious. You will become unreal. Underneath your ego mask, you will become very unhappy. If this happens to you, being gay will have become a hindrance. But you always get another chance, of course. Acute unhappiness can be a great awakener."

What we need, I think, is a Second Coming Out. The freedom we felt after our first coming out from mainstream society's expectations of us can, indeed, be felt again when we come out of our need to conform to gay society's expectations and standards.

You already know this - that the magnificent person you are is not based on how much hair you have on your head or how little of it you have on your body. That it doesn't really matter how tan your skin is or how white your teeth are, nor are those $200 jeans going to bring you any more inner peacefulness than a pair of basic Levi's.

If we already know this, why do we still take part in this endless rat race to fit in and feel accepted? I speak from experience, as I began undergoing that acute unhappiness to which Tolle was referring, because I had fallen asleep to the Truth of who I was.

"Nothing will be done through striving or vainglory," says Scripture, and I found that when I stopped trying so hard to be a worldly success and to make things happen for myself, and when I simply "Let go and let God," somehow the Universe became helpful and cooperative, and I became deeply peaceful.

I also had another Aha! moment when I realized that the people I really admired and most wanted to emulate were those who spent most of their time building up their Spiritual selves (by daily mediation, prayer, spiritual reading, doing service for others) instead of putting the focus on building up their physical selves or their stock portfolios or accomplishing some goal that would only be of benefit to them.

When I thought about these people (some well-known spiritual writers and teachers, and others in my own life who are not famous), I realized how beautiful they were - not in the supermodel ways of the world, but in the illumination of their Spirit.

A Course in Miracles affirms, "I am not a body. I am free. I hear the Voice that God has given me, and it is only this my mind obeys."

Think of it like the GPS system in your car. When

you're lost, you rely on it to guide you to your destination. Well, you have a Divine GPS inside you, but you need listen to it and to trust where it leads. It will guide you on the right path of your life's ultimate fulfillment.

That's what it means to Trust, to surrender to the Spirit. Thomas E. Powers says it is a "giving up of the egotistical, self-centered notion that I can direct and run my own life effectively and well...without conscious co-operation with the Spirit Within."

We see the importance of this in most faith systems and schools of thought. The word "Islam," for example, means "submission to God" and followers are called "Muslims," meaning "one who submits." The Bhagavad Gita, one of the most important Hindu scriptures, also urges its followers to "surrender your life to God."

Mahatma Gandhi, too, taught that renunciation means absence of hankering after fruit, and, yet, he who renounces reaps a thousand fold.

So, does that mean we're just supposed to sit back and go along for the ride? In a sense, yes. If you are seriously practicing your *G.I.F.T.*edness, the Law of Attraction will bring people and situations into your life which will help facilitate your greatest growth.

The wise choices you will make will be characterized by humility and service and gentleness. You will esteem others better than yourself. You will not be basking in the spotlight, but shining it on others. These are all the qualities the world and our egos tell us will not make us a success, when, in Truth, these qualities are at the heart of our very essence.

When you practice gratitude and meditation, you open yourself up to an abundant life. You will be given everything you need for your life's journey, and you will accomplish great things ("even greater things" than Jesus, he promised us) and experience a deep serenity and peace of mind. This is true success.

The Spirit inside you always knows what's best, so listen to its Wisdom through meditation and by keeping your thoughts in the present moment. Put your trust in its guidance.

When I was learning to surrender, a friend suggested asking the Spirit for a sign that I was on the right path. As someone more further along on the spiritual path, she could see that I was still a "doubting Thomas" about all of this. She told me that angels love to play, so make it something specific. Trust in it, she said.

I was still in enough pain that I decided to give it a try. During meditation, I visualized finding a nickel in an unexpected place. To make it even more specific and a surety that this sign would be just for me, I visualized this nickel having the year of my birth on it.

I focused on seeing this nickel in my mind's eye throughout the day. As the weeks went on, I'd come across the occasional quarter or pennies on the ground, but never a nickel. After a few months went by, I was beginning to lose hope, until one day, when I was packing for a trip to go visit my parents in Florida, I opened up my suitcase, and there was a lone nickel sitting inside it.

With anticipation, I held it up to my face and saw the year of my birth on it! The realization made me literally gasp my breath. As I continued looking at the nickel, I noticed the words "In God We Trust" and "Liberty" written on the front. Then, turning it over, "E Pluribus Unum" on the back, which, as you may know, is Latin for "Out of Many, One."

I thought a lot about those words over the next few days. Putting one's trust in Spirit leads to liberty - free of the chains of the ego, and, though we are many, we are all of the One True Spirit, which reminded me of the men I met at the clinical trial. When I saw myself in them, I was on my way to true freedom, the freedom which comes when we begin to grasp the concept of Oneness. Ego wants us to feel separate from one another. The Spirit teaches that we are all the same.

I've carried that nickel with me since that day, and I've never come across another nickel with the year of my birth on it since. If you're a skeptic like I was, I urge you to ask the angels to come out and play. I'd love to hear your stories and share them on the *Gay is a Gift* website (www.gayisagift.com).

Another thing that really helped me in my practice of Trust is a music CD I found for $2.49 on a Walgreen's clearance rack. (The Spirit knew that this was the only way a frugal guy like me would buy it!). This wonderful CD is Olivia Newtown-John's "Grace and Gratitude." If *Gay is a Gift* were to have an official soundtrack album, it would be this one.

While I was writing this book, I listened to "Grace and Gratitude" almost every morning as part of my meditation, and it always brought me to tears. Olivia Newton-John "gets it," having put much of what we've been discussing into practice in her own life.

The quote which began this section on Trust is a lyric from one of the songs on the CD, which is appropriately titled, "Let Go, Let God." Olivia's influences on this CD range from Deepak Chopra to Caroline Myss to Saint Francis of Assisi. Plus, Olivia wears the seven chakra colored bracelets on the CD cover.

I'm so grateful that the work of her Spirit served as inspiration to my own, and I encourage you to put "Grace and Gratitude" into your own life, too.

On one of her earlier songs, "Trust Yourself" (from another great CD called "Gaia"), Olivia sings: *"You know all the answers, they're all there inside you/ they've been there forever, just show them some Light."*

I'll end this section on Trust with some more wisdom from Mark Anthony Lord. In his book, *The Seven Living Words*, he writes, "Spirit, God, the greatness within knows what is required of us and what needs to be released.

The Holy Spirit will never mislead us, and the more we surrender to this truth, the more we will be able to hear and obey its inspiration and divine direction."

"Freedom comes when you learn to let go. Creation comes when you learn to say no. Do you wanna go Higher?"
- "The Power of Good-bye" by Madonna

The Tao of Madonna

Since this is a book on spirituality, you may think that the Madonna I'm referring to here is the Mother of God, but I'd like to talk about the one-time "Material Girl," Ms. Ciccone. Don't laugh. I'm being serious here.

Ever since Madonna hit the music scene back in the nineteen eighties, she has become an icon in the gay community, and, throughout her career, she has used spiritual imagery in her music, interweaving the sexual with the spiritual.

In recent years, Madonna has embraced Kabbalah, a discipline and school of thought concerned with the mystical aspects of Judaism, and its influence can be seen in much of her recent music, as far back as "Die Another Day," which is about dying to the ego. In fact, the Hebrew tattoo she wears on her arm in the video symbolizes the elimination of the ego.

In the song quote which begins this section, Madonna seems to be referring to the freedom that comes from surrendering to the ego, and how creation (Life) comes when we say no to it. This will bring us higher in consciousness.

We heard at the start of this book that all spiritual teachings originate from the same Source, so I'd like to encourage you to find out more about belief systems and schools of thought other than your own. When we do so, we begin to see that the same Spirit dwells in each one of us, even though our rituals and practices may look quite different. My understanding of Kabbalah has really helped me in uncovering my *G.I.F.T.*edness.

It's easy to see why Madonna and other celebrities like Demi Moore and Ashton Kutcher would be drawn to Kabbalah, as much of it has to do with extricating one's self from the grips of the ego's hold. If you and I have difficulty dealing with ego, imagine what it must be like for a celebrity! The red string bracelet many Kabbalahists wear is a reminder to act with humility. Demi's daughter, Rumor Willis, even has the words "Be Present" tattooed on her body.

Kabbalahists refer to ego as the "desire to receive for self alone" and see it as the source of all our pain and suffering. In Michael Berg's book *Becoming Like God: Kabbalah and Our Ultimate Destiny,* he uses a wonderful anecdotal story to explain our separation from Spirit:

A group of souls came down to Earth on a long ladder. Once they descended, they became human, causing them sadness, because they knew this signaled their separation from Spirit.

As the days and months progressed, they kept jumping into the air trying to grab the bottom rung of the ladder in hopes of climbing back up and reconnecting with their Spirits.

Some jumped for a little while, but soon gave up and settled in human existence. Others jumped for much longer, many years in fact, but they too failed to reach the bottom rung of the ladder.

One person, though, kept jumping and never stopped. Finally, the Spirit picked him up and brought him back home.

Some may see this person as Jesus, others maybe Buddha or another great spiritual teacher, but the message of

Berg's parable applies to you. Are you content to simply settle with the masses of the unfulfilled? Or - as Madonna sings in her song "Jump" - *Are you ready to jump?*

That song was part of the soundtrack for the film *The Devil Wears Prada,* which is very fitting as its lyrics speak of escaping our attachment to ego - our desire to receive for self alone - and returning to our true self - the Spirit, which is really our true nature.

The desire to receive for self alone is established in us as babies, as our wants and needs are tended to around the clock.

This continues into childhood, as many of us are brought up by well-meaning parents and teachers who stress to us that we are uniquely special individuals. Walk into the children's clothing section of any department store, and you'll see novelty tee-shirts for kids with messages like, "It's All About Me!" or "Baby Diva!" These shirts may seem funny, cute, even harmless, but think about the messages they're sending.

Then in grade school, we're taught both academically and on the playing field that competition is good. We must strive to win, to be number one, for ego tells us that our value lies in our accomplishments and achievements, as demonstrated by the "My Child's An Honor Student" bumper stickers on parents' cars.

In adolescence, though, is where ego really seems to sink its clutches into us. Wearing designer clothes or belonging to a certain social group determines our value in the eyes of others. The MTV reality show "My Super Sweet Sixteen" demonstrates this to a horrifying extreme, where teens feel entitled to be honored on their special birthday with the best gifts and parties their parents' money can buy. And if it's a nose job or bigger breasts that will do the trick, then so be it.

Our desire to receive for self alone, of course, carries into our adulthoods, where earning a certain income or having the right possessions determines our worth in the eyes of the world. Having learned our childhood lessons well, we defend our achievements with a sense of pride.

This reminds me of the parable of the young college graduate who approaches a wise elder and begins boasting about his accomplishments and plans for the future. "I've graduated at the top of my class, and I'm going to take a high-paying job a prestigious firm," he says proudly.

"And then what?" replies the elder.

"Well, then I'm going to get married to the most beautiful woman, and I'm going to buy an incredible house in a very desirable neighborhood."

"And then what?"

"Then I'm going to have children, and, of course, make sure they attend the best schools, so they, too, can achieve all these things."

"And then what?"

This continues a few more times, before the young man walks away in frustration, failing to comprehend the elder's questioning. Yes, the young man may go on to achieve much in the eyes of the world, but what of the Spirit?

"A sense of separation from God is the only lack you really need to correct," says *A Course in Miracles.* You must slay the ego if you wish to live a life of happiness, fulfillment and peace - an authentic life that only a true connection with the Spirit can bring.

Berg's book and another called *God Is A Verb* by Rabbi David A. Cooper have been so beneficial in helping me to understand that our ultimate peace can only come from union with our Source. Rabbi Cooper writes in his book, "Humility in Jewish mystical teaching means selflessness, the idea to let go of the trappings of self-identity, which include our desires, our expectations or aspirations. The practice for attaining this state is surrender."

And, Berg says, "When we go against our human nature, we're on the right road." Madonna also had a song called "Human Nature," and in it, she asks, "What was I thinking?" Remember this question whenever you are feeling stressed, anxious, fearful or angry. *What was I thinking to cause these feelings?* Whatever frequency you were on, trip the station, change the channel!

And, if you're still having trouble with trust, surrender, or slaying the ego, remind yourself of your connectedness with the Light by recalling the words of an earlier Madonna song, "Lucky Star":

> *"You make the darkness seem so far*
> *and when I'm lost you'll be my guide."*

Just turn around, and it's by your side. It's above you, beside you, within you and without you. Let that Light - that Divine GPS - be your guide.

S

"When you surrender completely to God, as the only truth worth having, you find yourself in service of all that exists. It becomes your joy and recreation. You never tire of serving others."   - Gandhi

SERVICE

Okay, we're not quite finished yet. I'm going to add an "S" to our acronym and make it plural. After all, we have been given many gifts.

The "S" in *G.I.F.T.S.* stands for Service. As we work on growing in consciousness, giving back seems the most natural response, for we're discovering that we reap what we sow, and when we give, we receive.

I love the quote from Mahatma Gandhi which begins this section, especially about how serving others becomes our recreation. We re-*create* (heal others, give them Life) every time we perform an act of service.

Amazingly, this doesn't feel like a burden, but a joy, for we discover that when we serve others, we uncover more of our Gay Gift.

Ram Dass says, "The very acts that we perform to relieve the suffering of another being, be they through offering a glass of water, holding a hand, building a road, or protesting against injustice, can also serve as a grist for the mill of our own spiritual growth, which, in turn, improves the effectiveness of our caring acts. It's like a self-sharpening appliance that improves with use."

We now know that when we think and send out peaceful thoughts, we receive peace in return. The peace prayer attributed to Saint Francis of Assisi beautifully explains what our service needs to be.

Where there is hatred, we'll send thoughts of love. Where there is darkness, we'll send out our Light.

All of us are called to be instruments of peace, but, as we've seen, gay people are endowed with special gifts that enable us not only to excel in this arena, but to teach others how to be peacemakers, as well, by seeking liberation for the benefit of all people.

Since we, ourselves, have experienced first-hand the pain of things like hatred and despair and doubt and falsehood, we now have the tools, the knowledge, the *GIFT* for giving love, hope, faith and truth to those who need them most.

It's why I suggested ending your gratitude journal entries each day with the words *"Now, How May I Serve?"* In writing these words, we are consciously asking the Universe to make us aware of opportunities for service to others each day and, by our asking, Spirit will show us how. (*Ask, and you shall receive*).

This does not mean that we have to do something amazingly great each day, something that will change the world. Mother Teresa of Calcutta said, "We cannot all do great things, but we can do small things with great love."

That said, I do believe these small acts of love do, indeed, change the world. As the Dalai Lama has said, "Love and compassion are necessities, not luxuries. Without them, humanity cannot survive. With them, we can make a joint effort to solve the problems of the whole of humankind."

Your small acts of service are, indeed, transforming the world. Put a small cupcake on a co-worker's desk with a cheerful note, shovel snow in an elderly neighbor's driveway, or help out a stranger whose car is stranded at the side of the road. You will perform these tasks with joy, for you'll be recreating (re-*creating),* and with passion (for you'll be showing com-*passion).*

The column I write for a local newspaper does not earn me much money, but when I learned that each small check I received for writing a column could pay for a year's school supplies for an entire classroom in an African grade school, I saw a way I could be of service in my own small way. Now, each time I write a column, I'm thinking about those kids.

Service for others can also be done simply by praying for them. Like with Dr. Emoto's work with ice crystals, we've seen the impact our thoughts and our words have on creation. So, when you sit quietly at prayer and send out thoughts of peace and healing to persons or countries in need, you are performing a great service in a small way.

When we pray, it's important to also send our Light to those who oppose and oppress us, to the political and religious leaders who openly speak out against gay people. As Jesus prayed on the cross, say, "Forgive them, for they know not what they do," and then continue to work to raise their awareness.

Often times, I pray for gay people in other countries who do not have the freedoms I do to express their love and their truth, and sometimes I focus on the words on my Vision Board: "Teach Others What We Know." The book you're now reading and holding in your hands was created in loving service by the Spirit within me, and I trust it will inspire yours.

In *Conversations with God*, Neale Donald Walsch writes, "Your job on earth is not to learn (because you already know), but to re-member who you are, and to re-member who everyone else is. That is why a big part of your job is to re-mind others, so they can re-member also. All the wonderful spiritual teachers have been doing just that. It is your sole purpose. Your soul purpose."

We must be careful, however, to be sure we're truly

working on re-membering ourselves before we seek to re-mind others. It's like the safety advice you hear before a flight (higher consciousness): "Be sure your own oxygen mask is secure, before you help others with theirs."

For example, in the Hindu tradition where it originated, yoga is all about dismantling the ego, but just because someone is teaching the practice today at a trendy big-city yoga center, it doesn't necessarily mean that he/she is spiritually pursuing the task.

The Alchemist writer, Paulo Coelho, tells the story of a monk who was meditating in the desert, when a beggar came up to him and asked for something to eat.

The monk was annoyed that the beggar had disturbed his meditation and said, "Go ask someone else. Can't you see I'm trying to commune with the angels?"

In response, the beggar said, "God placed himself lower than men, washed their feet, gave His life, and no one recognized Him. He who says he loves God - who doesn't see - and forgets his brother - who does see - is lying." And he turned into an angel. "What a pity, you almost made it," he remarked before leaving.

There are angels in our midst each and every day, but we must be keen enough to recognize them and our opportunities to serve. The good news is that the more we work on uncovering our *GIFT*endess, the more these opportunities will be made manifest to us.

Now, how may YOU serve?

After Saint John of the Cross broke through to my soul that afternoon in my basement, I found myself receiving signs from the Spirit everywhere.

While reading Eckhart Tolle's *A New Earth* in a doctor's waiting room, a nice woman approached me, asked how I was enjoying the book, and then suggested that I might enjoy reading Eric Butterworth, too, a writer with whom I was unfamiliar.

When I got back home, I received an email from the editor of the newspaper for which I contribute, and she was writing to see if I was interested in doing a story on a minister in my town who was retiring after many years of service. I agreed to do it.

I met the minister at her church, which was called Unity. As we sat in one of the pews with my small voice- recorder going, she told me all about Unity and their school of thought.

On my way out of the church after we had finished the interview, she handed me some literature about Unity, which she thought would be helpful for writing my article.

When I got back home, I noticed that one of the pamphlets she gave me was written by Eric Butterworth! As I read his words, they, too, were about what Saint John had been trying to teach me. Butterworth wrote, "The personal ego, the material-centered thoughts must go, must die so that the true essence of the divine in man may live."

After I submitted the article to the editor, I decided to attend a Unity service one Sunday. There, I was surprised to see gay and lesbian couples holding hands and taking part in the service. The minister's words were so "right on" with what I needed to hear that I literally had to hold myself back from breaking down into tears during her sermon.

Later, in the church bulletin, I read a notice about a lecture on Saint John of the Cross, believe it or not, that would be held the following week at something called "Mother's Trust" in a nearby town. This couldn't be a coincidence, I thought to myself, so I knew I'd have to attend.

Of course, I've later come to understand that there are no coincidences. This well-ordered Universe of ours knows exactly what we each individually need in order to help us awaken to the truth of our Divinity. All we need to do is send the message that we're open to receiving it.

Mother's Trust, I discovered, was an interfaith center in a town called Ganges, which I found highly appropriate since that's the name of the river in India which Hindus hold sacred, a river that facilitates the attainment of salvation. Again, no coincidences.

At the lecture on Saint John of the Cross, I was profoundly moved by the dramatic reading of one of his most famous poems, "Dark Night of the Soul." In the poem, John envisions sneaking out in the middle of the night and meeting up with Jesus in secret. Upon John's chest, Jesus rests his head, while John caresses him and parts his locks.

John ends the poem with "My face I reclined on the Beloved...and I abandoned myself, leaving my cares forgotten."

Through this gentle and loving scene of intimacy between two men, I came to more fully understand the peacefulness that can be felt when we truly sneak away from the false self and intimately unite with our true Spirit. We must embrace our gay giftedness in order to find true peace.

At subsequent visits to Mothers Trust, I began to learn more about this interfaith center which had been right in my backyard this whole time. The center supports people of many faith traditions in promoting peace and is dedicated in honoring and exploring the Motherhood of God, the feminine.

In the coming weeks following the lecture, spiritually-themed books found their way to me in interesting circumstances. One was left in a nightstand of one of the rooms in our bed-and-breakfast. Another was sent to me by the publisher of my first book, asking me for a blurb. And a third came to me when I was house-sitting for a vacationing neighbor and noticed it on his bookshelf.

Afterwards, I asked this neighbor if he had read the book I had discovered on his shelf, and he said that no, he hadn't. He just bought it for fifty-cents at a flea market, because he likes the look of old books, but he agreed to give it to me because I liked it so much.

Each of these books was a spiritual tome, and the insights I gained from reading each one were transforming. Again, it was no surprise that the recurring theme of each was the elimination of ego leading to the awakening of Spirit.

I thought back on the experiences I had had in the past few years, from the publication of my first book to working on movie sets and appearing on television, and I discovered that I was indeed the "Doubting Thomas" my friend had later pegged me as.

Just as Thomas doesn't believe that the other apostles have seen the risen Jesus (or, metaphysically speaking, have experienced Christ-consciousness for themselves), I didn't believe that the answer to my misery was in the reconnection with my Spirit until I was actually shown it.

Thomas needed to put his hands into Jesus' side before he finally "got it," and I needed the Universe to show me - to give me those experiences of the world - so that I would come to see that the things I had been seeking were not the things that were bringing me Life.

I'm grateful for the many teachers (quoted throughout this book) whom the Spirit has brought my way in the form of many wonderfully wise books. Recently, as I was writing my name on the inside front cover of one of those books (I was lending it out and wanted to make sure it would get back to me), I came to another Aha! realization of the Spirit.

My first name, Salvatore, means "Salvation," and my last name, Sapienza, means "Wisdom." As I wrote my name on this book which had, indeed, brought me these qualities, the Spirit seemed to be whispering to me, *"Now, it's your turn, Salvatore Sapienza,"* encouraging me to pass it on - not the actual book, per se, but the wisdom I was learning.

Just as these many other writers had helped me on my spiritual path, I was being called by name (*"I have redeemed you. I have called you by name,"* says God in Isaiah) to use my own gifts as a writer to assist in bringing this knowledge and salvation to others. Hence, the genesis for this book.

Which led me, oddly enough, to Genesis, the first book of the Bible. At Mother's Trust and Unity, I gained much spiritual wisdom concerning the feminine nature of the Spirit and my own gay giftedness. I also learned to look at the Bible metaphysically.

I'm amazed how many Christians today still take the Bible literally. Most Jews and Buddhists and Hindus I know read the stories of their ancient texts symbolically, and see metaphorically the eternal wisdom that's being shared. Jesus, himself, taught in parables.

This is why, many years back, I had dismissed the Old Testament from holding any wisdom for me, which is why I was so shocked to find Spirit leading me to Genesis of all places!

In reading the story of the creation of the world in Genesis, I was comforted by God's first words: "Let there be Light!" for, as I had been discovering, that Light is our true nature.

As for the creation of man, Genesis reads, "In the image of God, he created him, male and female," implying to me that not only is the Divine within us, but that it is also male *and* female. This may be one of the reasons why the Native

Americans upheld the "Two Spirits" as Holy (or Whole-y), as gayness transcends the polarity of male and female, bringing us closer to conscious awareness of the Divine.

It was only after eating from the tree of knowledge (the mind, the ego) that man became separated from God, so I came to understand, once again, that our job is to eradicate that knowledge.

The Cloud of Unknowing is the name of one the classic spiritual books that I had also recently read. Written by an anonymous English monk during the fourteenth century, the book teaches that it is only in the "unknowing" that we remember our union with the Divine.

I came to understand from the Genesis story that after the separation from God, man's God-given male/female nature was also split. Therefore, I concluded, it would only be in the reconciliation of these two natures where we'd once again become whole or holy.

Gay is a Gift sprang from that insight. Our nature as gay people is not a curse, but a Divine blessing! It doesn't make us "better" or "more special" than others, but it places us at an advantage in terms of spiritual growth, and it urges us to use that advantage to teach others what we know.

What a shame it would be to waste that gift by not allowing it to reach its full potential. When we practice our *G.I.F.T.*edness - *Gratitude, Inspiration, Forgiveness and Trust* - we not only begin to grow in our own awareness of ourselves as Divine Light, but we can then shine it on the world - *Service* - and assist others in uncovering their own giftedness.

Yet, it's important to remember what its says in the *Bhagavad Gita.* Krishna, who represents higher wisdom, says, "Only the fool whose mind is deluded by egotism considers himself to be the doer." And, as I've learned at Unity, it is not I, but the Christ-consciousness within, which does the work.

Therefore, I have great hope in the future. I envision a future world where families and communities will embrace and uphold gay people as Holy men and women, whose gifts will be esteemed and revered and held sacred. I see a world where parents celebrate their gay child's coming out day - a day of new Life - with a celebration! A future where governments and churches respect and listen to the wisdom of its gay constituents, and a planet where the peace of Oneness reigns.

We may not be able to make this future a reality in the blink of an eye, but we can hasten its progress by doing what it takes to present our present (our *GIFT*) to the world starting right here and now. It is our Divine mission.

<u>About the Wrist Band</u>

I hope that looking at the gift box you created - whether it sits atop your desk or on your nightstand or in some other prominent spot in your home or office - will be a gentle reminder for you to reconnect with your Spirit each time you look at it.

I realize, however, that there will be moments when you'll be stuck in traffic, or waiting in line at the grocery store, or sitting in a doctor's waiting room, or at the flight gate of an airport where your gift box won't be in sight.

And, it can be during these sometimes stressful moments when we need to be reminded of our Spirits more than ever. I began to think what I could do to create a visual that would always be in my sight; a visual that would remind me to shift my negative thinking and remain in the present Now moment every time I looked at it.

I thought about tattooing "Be Here Now" (after Ram Dass's famous book) on my forearm - to remember that this peace was always "at hand." Luckily, (to the relief of my partner, Gregg) I, instead, was inspired to create the "Gay is a Gift" wristband.

It's just like those charity yellow wristbands that were popularized a few years back by cyclist and Tour de France winner, Lance Armstrong, for the fight against cancer, and more recently, by Unity minister and writer, Will Bowen, who created the Complaint-free wristband as a reminder to stay positive.

The "Gay is a Gift" wristband is rainbow-colored, of course, and is embossed with the words "Gay is a Gift" on it. It's available for purchase by visiting this book's website (www.gayisagift.com).

It is my hope that by wearing this wristband each day, you'll be reminded of all the wisdom you've gleaned from this book (though, really, it's wisdom you've gleaned from inside yourself, right?), and that it will assist in keeping you grounded in the present moment (which is where Spirit lives) each time you look at it.

May the wristband on your arm also inspire others to do the same. Wearing it, I'm sure friends, colleagues, family members and strangers will ask you for an explanation as to what the wristband symbolizes, providing you with a blessed opportunity to pass on your wisdom, pass on your Light, pass on your Gift.

EPILOGUE:

The Tao of Madonna, Part II:

I couldn't possibly conclude this book without telling you about my experience with Madonna, but, this time, I'm referring to the Feminine Face of God.

A neighbor of ours recently gave us a box of some leftover slate he had, because he thought we could use it around our pond. After my partner and I had removed all the rocks and placed them around the pond, we noticed there was something shiny and silver at the bottom of the box.

It was a miraculous medal of Mary, the Mother of Jesus. I knew this medal well, as I remembered from my Catholic schooling that St. Catherine had designed this medal after hearing in meditation the words, "God wishes to charge you with a mission. You will be contradicted, but do not fear; you will have the grace to do what is necessary."

Retuning the box to our neighbor - a young man of Jewish heritage - we asked if the medal was his. He told us no and to keep it for ourselves. My partner, Gregg, who is not a religious man, decided to wear it around his neck on a chain and hasn't taken it off since.

A short time later, our elderly cat got sick on a large area rug in our office. The rug could not be saved, so we took all the furniture off it and began rolling it up. As we rolled up the area rug, we noticed something shiny and silver on the hardwood floor beneath it - a miraculous medal.

Instinctively, Gregg reached for the chain around his neck, and the medal he had been wearing was still there. This was now a second miraculous medal.

This was extremely odd, as neither one of us had ever had such a thing in our possession, and the office was completely bare when we purchased the house years back.

Now, I've always been very skeptical and uneasy when I've heard stories of people seeing the Virgin Mary in a Dunkin' Donut or something. In fact, I made fun of such people in my first book, *Seventy Times Seven*, but this was just too much of a coincidence, and I was beginning to learn that there are no coincidences.

I considered that maybe the feminine nature of the Spirit was trying to make itself known to me, and because of my Catholic upbringing, it came in the form of Mary. Had I been raised Jewish, maybe I would have experienced Shekhina, the feminine presence of God.

Gay writer and mystic, Andrew Harvey, says he came to his spiritual growth when he met Mother Meera, an avatar of the Divine Mother, and many relate to Spirit of Nature or Mother Earth.

So, I decided that maybe it would be a good idea for me to bring all this to my morning meditation. I searched the internet for an image of Mary that I could print out and place next to my candle.

All of the images I was finding were the very typical pious images of Mary, but then I came across an abstract painting of her, done all in yellows except for a blue butterfly in the center. The painting is by a contemporary German artist named Georg Kiehn, who writes in his online biography about Spirit and creation and finding God.

After printing out a small copy of the painting, I was intrigued with the blue butterfly, so I did an internet search on it. I discovered that the blue butterfly is a symbol for Mary. I came across countless stories on the internet of people seeing blue butterflies and feeling her presence. One woman poignantly writes about praying to Mary before undergoing surgery for a brain aneurysm. When she awakened, there in her room was a blue butterfly-shaped balloon someone had brought her. Later, a young nurse came in to check on her, and the woman was stunned. The nurse was wearing a smock that was filled with blue butterflies!

This got me thinking about butterflies, and it reminded me of a story I had heard once about a young boy who was watching a cocoon. He could see that the creature inside was struggling to get out, so the boy took a pair of scissors and cut the cocoon open in order to help the butterfly emerge. Sadly, the butterfly's wings were not yet strong enough, and it died outside the cocoon.

I came to see my spiritual growth that way. I was still in the cocoon, and that was okay. That was precisely where I needed to be - still forming, but I'd emerge and fly when the time was right.

The next morning, I placed the image of Mary and the blue butterfly next to my candle for morning meditation. That very afternoon, another dear neighbor of ours, a gay woman named Mary, believe it or not, asked if we might want a set of old mugs she no longer needed.

When I went to pick up the box of mugs from her a short time later, I gasped when I pulled the first one out. The design on the mug was of blue butterflies!

Now, I have rolled my eyes at stories like this in the past from seemingly narcissistic and unbalanced people claiming authorization by God. Please understand that my intention in sharing this epilogue is to not to make such claims, but to demonstrate to you how to live a life that is full of miracles by seeing miracles all around you. When you begin to open yourself to the Spirit, you begin to look at the world symbolically and notice the profound significance of things that have always been right before your eyes.

For example, one morning, I had been reading about Henri Nouwen's love for sunflowers. He had a framed print of Van Gogh's painting "Vase with Flowers" above the desk where he wrote his many books, as he found sunflowers inspiring. Nouwen said that each flower is imperfect, but taken together, they're perfection.

Later that day, I was running errands in town and came across a small book sale set up in someone's garage. On the lawn out front stood a six-foot tall metal sculpture of a sunflower.

As I browsed the books in the garage, there was a copy of one of Nouwen's books! As I went to pay for it, I remarked how much I liked the metal sunflower sculpture.

"You want it?" asked the bookseller. "It's for sale, too." So, I purchased the book and the sunflower. The sculpture now sits outside the window where I write, and - thinking of Nouwen's desire to write a book about homosexuality one day - it provided me with inspiration as I wrote this book.

That's what I mean about looking at the world symbolically and seeing miracles everywhere.

Maybe you're a "doubting Thomas" like I am, and need to be shown signs, so ask for them. Or maybe you're one the blessed who believe without seeing.

Either way, I know now that when we are ready, Spirit, in whatever guise it may take, will show us the signs we best need at each step of our spiritual growth. Be watchful for them, and know how truly special you are to receive them. They are a gift, and so are you!

I am so grateful for you, and I hope you will share your stories with me and others on the *Gay is a Gift* website (www.gayisagift.com). In this way, we can create a global support group and nurture one another as we venture along on our spiritual journeys, separately, yet together as One.

"How could anyone ever tell you,
you are anything less than
beautiful?

How could anyone ever tell you,
you are less than whole?

How would anyone fail to notice
that your loving is a miracle?

How deeply you're connected
to my soul."

- Libby Roderick

ABOUT THE AUTHOR

Salvatore Sapienza is a former monk in the Catholic Church and the author of **Seventy Times Seven**, which was nominated for two Lambda Literary Awards, including Best Spirituality.

During his years in religious life, Sapienza worked alongside Father Mychal Judge in helping to establish St. Francis AIDS Ministry, one of the first Catholic AIDS organizations in the country. Sapienza writes about his friendship with Father Judge, "The Saint of 9/11," in the anthology entitled **Queer and Catholic**.

As a writer, Sapienza's work has appeared in *The Gay and Lesbian Times*, *Ashe Journal*, and *The Holland Sentinel* newspaper, among others. He has done speaking engagements at numerous schools, retreat centers and bookstores around the country and has appeared on Public Television and National Public Radio.

He and his partner own and operate a bed and breakfast in Saugatuck, a gay-friendly resort town on Lake Michigan. For more, please visit www.gayisagift.com

<u>RESOURCES</u>

The following is a partial list of the books and music which have assisted me along my spiritual journey and in the writing of *Gay is a Gift*.

It is my hope that one or more of the writers quoted in this book have inspired you to want to learn more, and that you will seek out their books.

I invite you to share additional names of the resources which have helped you by posting them on the *Gay is a Gift* website: www.gayisagift.com.

<u>BOOKS</u>:

The Power of Now, by Eckhart Tolle (1999) Namaste Publishing

A New Earth: Awakening to Your Life's Purpose, by Eckhart Tolle (2005) Plume Press

Becoming Like God: Kabbalah and Our Ultimate Destiny, by Michael Berg (2004) Kabbalah Publishing

God is a Verb: Kabbalah and the Practice of Mystical Judaism, by David A. Cooper (1997) Riverhead Books

John of the Cross: Man and Mystic, by Richard P. Hardy (2004) by Paulist Press

The Seven Living Words, by Mark Anthony Lord (2008) by Accelerator Books

Discover the Power Within You, by Eric Butterworth (1968) by Harper San Francisco

Wounded Prophet: A Portrait of Henri J.M. Nouwen, by Michael Ford (1999) Image Books

Father Mychal Judge: An Authentic American Hero, by Michael Ford (2002) Paulist Press

Abandonment to Divine Providence, by Jean-Pierre de Caussade, translated by John Beevers (1975) First Image Books

Conversations with God, by Neale Donald Walsh (1996) Putnam Books

This Remarkable Gift: Being Gay and Catholic, by Father Maurice Shinnick (1997) St. Leonard's Press, Australia

First Questions on the Life of the Spirit, by Thomas E. Powers (1959) Harper & Row

A Prophet in His Own Land: A Malcolm Boyd Reader, edited by Bo Young and Dan Vera (2008) Lethe Press

Compassion in Action: Setting Out on the Path of Service, by Ram Dass and Mirabai Bush (1992) Bell Tower Books

Coming Out Spiritually, by Christian de la Huerta (1999) Tarcher Press

The Spirit of Intimacy, by Sobonfu Somé (2000) Harper

Sex As God Intended by John J. McNeill (2008) Lethe Press

Gay Spirit: Myth and Meaning by Mark Thomspon (1998) St. Martin's Griffin

The Hidden Spirituality of Men: Ten Metaphors to Awaken the Sacred Masculine , by Matthew Fox (2009)

The Four Agreements: a Practical Guide to Personal Freedom - A Toltec Wisdom Book, by Don Miguel Ruiz (1997) Amber-Allen Publishing

Gay Perspective: Things Our Homosexuality Tells Us About the Nature of God and the Universe, by Toby Johnson (2008) Lethe Press

MUSIC

Surrender by Michael Gott (2008) Available on i-Tunes and at www.michaelgott.com. Michael's music is beloved in New Thought spiritual communities around the world, plus, he's one of us!

Grace and Gratitude by Olivia Newton-John (2006) ONJ Productions. Available on i-Tunes and at www.olivianewton-john.com

How Could Anyone by Libby Roderick (2005) Turtle Island Records. This CD contains the song "How Could Anyone," whose beautiful lyrics close out this book. She's one of us, too!

Meditations from Solitude by John Michael Talbot (1994) Troubadour Records. Meditative music set to the words of mystics like Clare and Francis of Assisi, John of the Cross and Thomas Merton. Available on i-Tunes and at www.johnmichaeltalbot.com

One With the World by David Ault (2005) The Conscious Company. Includes the song "I'm Here to Remind You," whose beautiful lyrics open this book.

OTHER

To learn more about:

Unity: www.unity.org

Science of Mind magazine: www.scienceofmind.com

Centers for Spiritual Living:
www.unitedcentersforspiritualliving.org

Easton Mountain: Gay retreat center in upstate New York:
www.eastonmountain.com

Spirit Journeys: Gay retreats at destinations all over the globe.
www.spiritjourneys.com

Printed in Great Britain
by Amazon.co.uk, Ltd.,
Marston Gate.